one girl can change the world

claudia mitchell & kim goad

D0066891

Standard®
PUBLISHING
Bringing The Word to Life

Cincinnati, Ohio

Published by Standard Publishing, Cincinnati, Ohio
www.standardpub.com

Acquisitions editor: Robert Irvin
Project editor: Kelli B. Trujillo
Cover and interior design: Jenette McEntire

Published in association with the literary agency of Credo Communications LLC, Grand Rapids, MI 49525; www.credocommunications.net.

ISBN 978-0-7847-2229-9

 Library of Congress Cataloging-in-Publication Data
Mitchell, Claudia, 1954-
 One girl can change the world / by Claudia Mitchell and Kim Goad.
    p. cm.
 Includes bibliographical references (p.   ).
 ISBN 978-0-7847-2229-9 (perfect bound)
1. Leadership--Religious aspects--Christianity. 2. Teenage girls--Religious life. 3. Christian teenagers--Religious life. 4. Self-actualization (Psychology) in adolescence. 5. Self-actualization (Psychology)--Religious aspects--Christianity. I. Goad, Kim, 1967- II. Title.
 BV4597.53.L43M58 2009
 248.8'33--dc22
                        2009008424

15 14 13 12 11 10 09   9 8 7 6 5 4 3 2

contents

one girl

dedication

This book is dedicated to . . .

. . . our mothers, Mary Kay Meadows and Pat Cain, who first and best modeled for us that One Girl *Can* Change the World.

. . . our fathers, James Goad and Dayle Cain, who encouraged us to be Princesses with Purpose.

. . . and the student leaders of Hilltop Christian Camp Girls' Week, who are forever amazing us with your world changing spirits.

acknowledgments

One Girl has seemed divinely orchestrated from the start—from the first unexpected brainstorming session at Starbucks® coffeehouse (where we chicken-scratched the outline on the back of a napkin) to the serendipitous way that God put the right people in our path at just the right times to help us along the way. Above all, we thank God in whom "we live and move and have our being." Lord, it has been our constant prayer that we would make *you* proud.

Our deep expressions of gratitude also to our agent, Tim Beals with Credo Communications, Inc. (Thanks for believing in us, Tim!); our editor, Kelli B. Trujillo (Thanks for your insights and enthusiasm—you definitely kicked the book up a notch . . . or two!); the team at Standard (who is anything *but* "standard"! Thanks for making our first navigation through the publishing world a blast!); John Mitchell of Monarch Media Studios (for late-night meetings at Steak 'n Shake and video shoots in the rain with a group of giggling girls!); and to our spiritual families at Sherwood Oaks Christian Church and South Union Christian Church for your constant love, support, and prayers.

And, most especially, thank you to our One Guys:

Claudia: Ken Mitchell—after thirty-eight years, you still make my heart skip a beat when you walk in the room!

Kim: David Shirley—for showing me that God is still in the business of surprises (who would've *thought?!*) . . . something wonderful is happening!

introduction

Can One Girl
Really Change the World?

Claudia: I stood in front of about a hundred girls at the Christian summer camp I've led for more than a decade, ready to deliver the morning prayer before breakfast. Each year I eagerly anticipate how God will show up and show off through the girls' lives. I don't remember the entire prayer I led that morning, but I remember part of it being something like this: "God, I'm looking out on this sea of girls who have the power to change the world!"

Afterward, on my way out, a student grabbed me by the arm. Ashleigh has a deep love for God and an intensely serious attitude about her relationship with him. She looked at me with wide brown eyes and asked, "Did you really mean that?" My mind was already distracted with the next item on the day's agenda. "Mean what?" Ashleigh clarified for me in almost a whisper, full of hope, "Can one girl **really** change the whole world?" Without hesitation I said, "Yes!" Then with one word she completely blew me away. She simply asked, *"HOW?"*

For years—as a teacher, a youth minister, and a girls camp leader—my life has been about developing young people, about believing that one girl **can** change the world. My life has been spent on the premise that we have a God who loves us deeply and desires that our lives really **mean** something. Jesus called us the light of this world (Matthew 5:14-16). And take a look at Psalm 139—God knew you when you were in your mother's womb. He knows your every thought. He sees where you are every moment of the day. He knows what you're going to say before you even say it. He is familiar with all your ways. He numbers the very hairs on your head (Matthew 10:30). And he has great plans for you! Ephesians 2:10 says, "For we are God's workmanship, created in Christ Jesus to do good works, which God prepared in advance for us to do." Yes, I believe one girl can change the world—because God's Word says so and because I've seen countless young women actually do it.

But Ashleigh's questions gnawed at me: **How** can one girl change the world? I came to realize that young women really need to know, in the innermost fiber of their beings, that they can change the world. And they need practical knowledge about how to do it. So that's why my friend Kim and I wrote this book . . .

Our guess is that you've picked up this book because you're asking the same questions Ashleigh asked. You long to know that you have a grander purpose and that God has gifted you with the ability and resources to see it through. Somewhere deep in your heart you have a secret hope that your life is meant to really *mean* something. Perhaps you're bored with life being about just getting through school and worrying about boys, what to wear, and how to gain popularity. You're tired of the status quo. You want *more* out of your life.

Or maybe you are hearing that still, small voice inside telling you there's more in store for you, but you also have your doubts: *Who . . . me? A leader? Ha! You don't know me. I'm not the leader type. I'm shy. I can't inspire people. I don't have any experience. And I have enough on my plate just trying to get through my day, let alone change the world.*

Or maybe you're already on board. You've got a suspicion that maybe, just maybe, you *could* do great things. Maybe you've even got an inkling already about what it is you're supposed to do . . . but you're not exactly sure how to go about it. Where should you start? You need some direction.

Which describes you? Do you believe you can change the world? We hope to convince you that you not only *can*, but you are *called* to. We're going to drive a stake in the ground once and for all on what God says about the matter. And we're going to help you get inspired along the way by stories of how other young women have changed their world—ordinary young women like you who had their own flaws and insecurities. Biblical women like Sarah, Hagar, Rahab, Hannah, Esther, Miriam, Mary the mother of Jesus, Mary of Magdala, and many others. Historical women who came along to take their own stand on God's time line, like Joan of Arc, Amy Carmichael, and Mother Teresa. And young women who are changing the world today, like our friends Ellen, Tori, Sylva, Lilly, and Kara.

These leaders have similar qualities . . . and very different ones too. Paul wrote in his letter to the Romans, "Just as each of us has one body with many members, and these members do not all have the same function, so in Christ we who are many form one body, and each member belongs to all the others" (12:4, 5). Yes, we'll learn about the general qualities that any good leader should have, but we'll also help you figure out what kind of leader *you* are and what specific passions or causes God has placed on *your* heart.

Once you get that you're called to be a leader and you understand what particular kind of leader you are and what your passion is, you need to know how to get there. Will Rogers, the late American humorist and actor, said, "Even if you're on the right track, you'll get run over if you just sit there."[1] So we'll talk about how to develop a solid plan and *start doing* what you're called to do. We'll talk about how to hear God speaking to you, how to acquire the skills you need, and how to align with other people who can help you get there.

Last, we'll talk about how you can tell if you're on the right track. Is the plan working? No attempt to achieve anything great is without its obstacles and setbacks. Expect them! People will fail you, circumstances will fail you, and sometimes you'll just plain fail yourself. But Thomas Edison said, "Many of life's failures are people who did not realize how close they were to success when they gave up." [2] So let's deal with the obstacles and setbacks head-on together.

Our Stories

Every so often you'll notice handwritten stories popping into chapters here and there (like at the start of this intro). We, Claudia and Kim, have written this book together out of our shared passion, and it's been a great experience to write as a team. But just like *your* life story is your own, we each have our own unique life stories and experiences we want to share with you. So when one of us has a story to tell you about something that's happened in just one of our lives, you'll see it printed in handwriting, just like a personal journal.

Speaking of Journals . . .

We've also put together the *One Girl Journal* for you, full of tools that will help you really dig into the content of these chapters and figure out for yourself exactly how God is uniquely calling you to change the world. If you can, get a copy of the *One Girl Journal* for yourself and follow along. Or you can turn a blank notebook *into* a journal—we'll tell you more about how to do that in chapter 2.

Get Your Shoes On

Actress Bette Midler once said, "Give a girl the correct footwear and she can conquer the world."[3] We couldn't agree more, so that's why we've included the "Get Your Shoes On!" questions for small group reflection at the end of every chapter in this book.

There's just something about slipping into the right pair of shoes that can totally transform us, isn't there? On any given day—like Dorothy's magical red shoes with the power to take her back home or Cinderella's slipper cinching the deal with her prince—the decision to wear flip-flops, clogs, or Mary Janes has less to do with what's practical and more to do with getting into character. We get ready for any occasion by primping, putting on the right outfit, and donning our matching accessories. But the thing we do when we're ready to leave the house—when we're ready to *move*—is to (*ah!*) slip into that perfect pair of shoes to complete the ensemble. Reading the following chapters will prepare your heart and mind. But the "Get Your Shoes On!" questions will prepare you for action. They're about moving from where you are to where you want to be.

So read this book with some of your best girlfriends or as part of a youth ministry small group at church—you'll grow individually and you'll get closer to each other as you take this world-changing challenge together. And if you don't have a small group to talk about this book with, then turn the questions into ideas for journaling your thoughts. However you go about it, we hope you do get your shoes on and "let every detail in your lives—words, actions, whatever—be done in the name of the Master, Jesus, thanking God the Father *every step of the way*" (Colossians 3:17, *The Message*, italics added).

Get To It!

Claudia: One of the biggest obstacles we face in life is procrastination. Oh, do I know all about procrastination! I've been meaning to clean my car out all week. Not exactly a world-changing endeavor, I know. But if you'd ever ridden in my car, you'd understand why no one ever expects to ride with me in a hurry. First, an assortment of books, CDs, loose papers, coffee cups, walking shoes, and the occasional empty fast food bag have to be picked up and thrown in the back to make room for the passenger. I'm not kidding you—a clean car is just not a priority in my life, so I procrastinate. But the other day, I drove a friend to lunch and, to my absolute horror and embarrassment, when she got out of my car I noticed a sticky milkshake lid stuck to her bottom. That's when I realized I'd procrastinated long enough!

We're so thrilled you're picking this book up now instead of waiting 'til you found yourself sitting in your own sticky situation! The Lord has great plans for you, and he's equipped you to do them . . . *and that changes everything.* So let's not waste any more time! Let's get to it!

part 1

Do I Know Who I Am?

> "Never doubt that a community of thoughtful,
> committed women, filled with
> the power and love of God,
> using gifts they have identified and developed,
> and pursuing passions planted in them by God—
> never doubt that these women
> can change the world."
> —Lynne Hybels, *Nice Girls Don't Change the World* [1]

1

a princess with a purpose

> "Me, a princess?"
>
> "You are the legal heir."
>
> "I never lead anyone."
>
> "We will help you to be a princess, to rule.
> If you refuse to accept the throne then the kingdom
> will cease to exist as we know it."
>
> —*The Princess Diaries* movie [1]

Let's face it—there's a lot of hype about princesses these days. Made popular by movies, books, and the retail industry (everything from pink T-shirts to pillows, tiaras, and wands), we are inundated with this whole business of princess-thinking. Little girls play dress-up in puffy chiffon dresses and plastic slippers, dreaming of their prince-to-come. From the time we are little, we read classics like *The Princess and the Pea, Cinderella, Snow White,* and *A Little Princess,* all with the theme that any girl—no matter what her circumstances—can become a princess.

So what about you? Are you a girl whose childhood dream was to be a princess . . . and does that dream still linger? Do you love girly-girl stuff—dressing up, styling your hair, and feeling beautiful? Or are you a girl who prefers soccer cleats over glass slippers and can hardly stand the sight of pink? Whether you're one or the other—or if you're somewhere in between—this book is for you!

We have to admit up front that in some senses we have a hard time relating to all the princess propaganda. Even as kids we weren't what you'd call girly-girls. In fact, we were more comfortable making mud pies, climbing trees, and playing sports with the boys in the neighborhood than pretending to be princesses. And today, as grown women, we're both more comfortable with a fly-fishing rod or a hiking stick in our hands than a sparkly wand. We prefer dressing up in fleece and walking in the woods to dressing up in ballroom gowns and waltzing. So you might think that we're the last people on earth qualified to talk about a girl's secret longing to be a princess. *Or are we?*

A Different Kind of Princess

There's a whole different image of a princess that we want to share with you, and it contrasts quite a bit with the world's view. When God says in Genesis 2:18 that he's going to make woman, the English translation we use says "I will make a helper" for the man, Adam. We don't know about you, but being labeled a "helper" doesn't exactly rev our engines! At first glance being a "helper" can sound unimportant, weak, and insignificant. But the actual Hebrew word used here is *ezer*, and its verb form *azar* means "to help, succour [sic], support."[2] *Succor* isn't a word that *anyone* uses anymore, and though it's a word from another era entirely, it has a powerful meaning: someone who provides assistance in times of great difficulty. *Ezer* is used twenty-one times in the Old Testament and is mostly used in military language in reference to soldiers and allies. Dr. Frank T. Seekins, in his booklet *A Mighty Warrior: The Hebrew-Biblical View of a Woman*, writes that "the Hebrew word picture [for *ezer*] clearly describes a military ally . . . who 'sees' the enemy."[3]

In other words, God's idea of a princess is a *warrior!* Though you live in a world that makes every attempt to lure your heart toward superficial things, as a princess in God's kingdom, God calls you to battle! He calls you to love radically, pray fervently, care for the poor, courageously confront injustice, and give sacrificially of your time, talents, and money. He has a battle plan, and it includes *you* as you defend and live out God's kingdom values.

In the following chapters, we'll journey together as you seek to discover God's specific marching orders for your life and learn how to execute them. How will you live as a warrior princess in a world that's in desperate need of your help? Is it in a broken home where you'll be an instrument of peace? Is it at school where you'll bridge gaps with the unloved? Is it in your community where you'll serve the poor in a soup kitchen? Or maybe it's like our friend Savanna, who's a champion NCAA swimmer—maybe God wants you to excel in your talents so that you'll have a platform from which you can display your faith. Wherever it is, God is calling you to live out his kingdom values as a warrior princess. So *bring it,* girl!

A New Name

You've probably heard about how God took Abram—this normal old guy living in a world that worshiped many pagan gods—and called him out of that world and made a promise to him that would impact all generations to come (even yours). God said, "You will be the father of many nations . . . I will establish my covenant as an everlasting covenant between me and you and your descendants after you for the generations to come, to be your God and the God of your descendants after you"

(Genesis 17:4, 7). At that point God renamed Abram "Abraham," which means "father of many."

This story about Abraham is pretty important, but did you know that when God renamed Abram, he also renamed Abram's wife, Sarai? The Bible says, "God also said to Abraham, 'As for Sarai your wife, you are no longer to call her Sarai; her name will be Sarah. I will bless her and will surely give you a son by her. I will bless her so that she will be the mother of nations; kings of peoples will come from her'" (Genesis 17:15, 16). Guess what the name *Sarah* means? It means *princess!* Let that soak in for a minute. The woman who God called "the mother of nations" and through whom he established his covenant is called "princess."

God didn't name Sarah "princess" because of anything remarkable or extraordinary she'd done. On the contrary, the Bible tells us about lots of mistakes Sarah made. Instead of trusting God, she laughed at God when she heard God tell Abraham that she would bear a child at the age of ninety; she tried to force God's plan by arranging for her husband to sleep with her servant; and then she was hateful and acted cruelly toward that servant and the resulting son when her plan worked.

Despite all this—despite her faults and failings—God still called Sarah "princess." Why? Because he chose to. Is it possible that God also calls *you* "princess" before you've earned the name? Could it be that he calls *you* "princess," not because of anything good or bad you've done, but because of what he envisions for you?

This is the God who knows the exact number of hairs on your head, who has you engraved in the palms of his hands, who says you are the apple of his eye, who made you in his image, who knew you before you were ever knit together in your mother's womb, and who loved you so much that he gave his only son for you. And at the end of time as we now know it, he's going to give you a new name—known only to you and to him (Revelation 2:17). We love how Nicole Johnson puts it in *Keeping a Princess*

Heart: In a Not-So-Fairy-Tale World:

> No one but God can recognize you fully.
>
> No one but God can love you so completely.
>
> No one but God can fulfill your heart's deepest desires.
>
> No one but God can name you Princess. [4]

Wow. What are you supposed to do with a love like that?

A Princess with a Purpose

Our friend Sandee describes herself as a longtime "princess wannabe." As a young girl Sandee grew up watching beauty pageants on TV and dreamed of becoming Miss Universe. She envied the winner for her sparkly crown and *oohed* and *ahhed* at the evening gown competitions. She'd say to herself, "Someday I want one of those crowns! I want to be beautiful . . . chosen . . . special." But as her junior high and high school years went by, her dream began to die. She had braces, she had acne—and Sandee began to realize that she didn't quite fit the ideal beauty-queen image.

Eventually things seemed to take a turn, and she found herself on her high school homecoming queen court. She prayed, "Please, God, you know this is my *only* chance! This is it!" But then she heard some painful gossip: someone was saying that she wasn't pretty enough to be homecoming queen. Sandee was hurt, but she also believed that God knew how much it meant to her, so she felt she still had a chance.

When homecoming night arrived Sandee didn't win. She came to this devastating conclusion: "Even God rejects me. God does not love me. I cannot trust God." For ten years after this heartbreak, Sandee struggled through rebellion against God and what she describes as self-imposed "heaps of preventable pain" as she battled anorexia and then bulimia.

When we think of Sandee's story, we picture the TV show *Cold Case*. Can't you just imagine a box being pulled from the archives with Sandee's name on it? A box containing evidence of the day her real self died? The date marked on the box would be the date she joined young women all over the world who feel fat and ugly and believe they can no longer trust their creator's view of them: "I am enthralled by your beauty. Honor me, for I am your Lord" (see Psalm 45:11). If we look deep enough into the box, we might find evidence of an apple, pointing all the way back to Eve, who listened to the whisper of the enemy when he told her, "You cannot trust God . . . God does not love you."

What about you? Have you believed the enemy? Perhaps as you're reading this book, you're also unpacking a box of lies from your own shelf. What is it that you have allowed the enemy to convince you about yourself? What lies, messages, or pressures have paralyzed you and prevented you from living as the amazing young woman God calls you to be?

The truth is that you are an incredible masterpiece crafted by the ultimate divine artist—God! You are a *wonder*. You have over two hundred bones and thousands of hairs on your head. Your thigh bones are stronger than concrete, and you replace several million blood cells every second. Even though you are made of 80 percent water, you can learn seven facts per second every second for the rest of your life . . . and still have room for more! No one in this world has your DNA, personality, or particular gifts.

When you hear those lies from the enemy, turn to God's Word and remind yourself of the truth! God made you as his princess, and he's given you a purpose. Check this out: "But you are a chosen people, a royal priesthood, a holy nation, a people belonging to God, that you may declare the praises of him who called you out of darkness into his wonderful light" (1 Peter 2:9). What it all boils down to is that your purpose is to declare God's praises. And how do you do that? You declare his praises with your life. You are called to impact this world *as only you can*. Your life was meant to be an adventure—not just something to "get through." You can become the leader you were born to be.

Just like Aslan in *The Chronicles of Narnia*, our God is on the move. And he intends for you to move with him. Pastor Erwin McManus puts it this way: "Jesus is transforming lives, writing history, creating the future, and unleashing the kingdom of God. If you plan to keep step with Jesus the Pioneer, you better expect some changes."[5] So what is it that God may be calling you to do to minister to your generation? How are you called to be a princess with a purpose?

Princesses in Disguise

Some of the best princesses of all time are the ones who are undercover. We don't find them sitting on thrones and wearing beautiful gowns, going "Hey, everybody! I'm a princess! Bow in my presence!" Cinderella is wearing rags and cleaning the fireplace. Snow White is hanging out with seven quirky little men. Danielle (in the movie *Ever After*) is working like a slave in her stepmother's home. Mia Thermopolis (from *The Princess Diaries*) is a regular high school student grappling with freshman algebra and making amends with her best friend. None of them needs the outer trappings of royalty; they carry in their hearts and in their characters their true identities as princesses. They are princesses in disguise.

The good news for many of us is this: princesses come in many different disguises, from girly-girls to tomboys. We don't all have the same talents, passions, or upbringings. We don't all have to wear pink! Ever hear the saying, "well-behaved women rarely change the world"? We're not suggesting that you begin behaving badly, but the point is a good one: girls who change the world aren't usually the ones who follow all of society's "rules."

Do you remember that scene in *Ever After* when Danielle (still a princess in disguise) and the prince are hiding in the woods and come face-to-face with a group of gypsies who threaten their lives? Danielle, dressed only in her undergarments because her dress has been slowing her down on the run, stands up to the leader of the gypsies and demands that he let her go. He tells her she can go away with anything she can carry. She asks, "May I have your word on that, sir?" He replies with a smirk, "On my honor as a gypsy, whatever you can carry." And she walks over to the prince, lugs him over her shoulders, and carries him away on her back. [6]

Don't you just love that? Here are these rough men who see this little thing in her undergarments, and they're totally mocking her; they don't really think she can carry much. But her courage and strength surprise them. She defies their expectations. She busts through their stereotypes. She breaks the rules.

Consider these real-life princesses in disguise who also broke a few of the rules:

- **Miriam**—Moses' sister and a prophetess, who led the people in worship after their deliverance from Egypt (Exodus 15). (God refers to her as one of the three core leaders of the exodus in Micah 6:4: "I brought you up out of Egypt and redeemed you from the land of slavery. I sent Moses to lead you, also Aaron and Miriam.")

- **Rahab**—who risked her life and committed treason against her government in order to hide the Israelite spies and was instrumental in the Hebrews' military strategy for winning the promised land (Joshua 2, 6).

- **Deborah**—the only female judge in the Old Testament, she led the Israelites in a successful military defeat of the Canaanites. Barak, the

Israelite military leader, refused to go into battle without Deborah (Judges 4, 5).

⑥ **Ruth**—who faced great heartache with courage, chose to leave her homeland behind to follow God (book of Ruth).

⑥ **Abigail**—she cunningly used her beauty and intelligence to bring peace to a conflict and prevent bloodshed (1 Samuel 25).

⑥ **Huldah**—a prophetess who boldly spoke God's truth to power (2 Kings 22:14-20).

⑥ **Esther**—who put her own life on the line in order to convince the king of Persia not to annihilate the entire Jewish race (book of Esther).

⑥ **Mary, the mother of Jesus**—as a young teenager, she risked her reputation and her marriage when, through God's miraculous work, she became pregnant with and gave birth to Jesus, the Son of God (Luke 1, 2).

⑥ **Lydia**—a businesswoman who opened up her home to Paul and his friends (Acts 16:11-15).

⑥ **Phoebe**—who helped Paul in his ministry in the early church (Romans 16:1, 2).

⑥ **Nympha and Apphia**—who both risked their lives to host the early church in their homes (Colossians 4:15; Philemon 2).

Amazing women like these aren't only found in the Bible—we see them in the pages of history. Consider the stories of these princesses in disguise:

⑥ **Joan of Arc**—she led the French army in the Hundred Years' War. Joan was burned at the stake when she was nineteen years old for claiming to have received visions from God.

⑥ **Sojourner Truth**—born into slavery, she became a leader in the Underground Railroad and is remembered as one of American history's best-known activists for abolition and women's rights.

⑥ **Clara Barton**—who delivered medical supplies and treated wounded soldiers on the battlefields of the Civil War and who later organized the American Red Cross.

- **Eliza Shirley**—who, as a seventeen-year-old British immigrant, was a bold evangelist and the first to bring the work of the Salvation Army to America.

- **Marie Monsen**—a soft-spoken Norwegian woman who served as a missionary in China in the 1930s and was instrumental in Christian revival there during a time of extreme persecution.

- **Mother Teresa**—who, among countless other accomplishments, once negotiated a temporary cease-fire between Israelis and Palestinians and crossed a war zone to rescue thirty-seven children trapped in a hospital.

- **Ruby Bridges**—who, as a six-year-old girl in 1960, marched through a crowd of racist protestors and became the first black child to attend her formerly all-white school.

How about women today—ordinary women like you or like us who are changing the world? There's Peggy Welch, our friend who impacts the world by using her influence as an Indiana state representative and also through her work as a nurse to cancer patients. There's Renée Altson, a young woman who overcame extreme abuse and has written a book (called *Stumbling Toward Faith*) to help others who've been abused. And there's our friend Doris who overcame addictions during her teen years and now uses her experiences to counsel others. We could go on and on—and you probably could too. Who are the princesses in disguise that you know?

These women from the Bible, from history, and from our everyday lives come from all different backgrounds—some poor, some prosperous; some educated, some not; some from loving and supportive parents, some from abusive families—yet each discovered the purpose for which she was uniquely created . . . and then got her shoes on and got to work!

In the classic book *A Little Princess,* by Frances Hodgson Burnett, the main character Sara's father has died, all his fortune has been taken, and she's been left penniless and sent to live in an attic. Despite these harrowing circumstances, Sara says something amazing: "Whatever comes . . . cannot alter one thing. If I am a princess in rags and tatters, I can be a princess inside. It would be easy to be a princess if I were dressed in a cloth of gold, but it is a great deal more of a triumph to be one all the time when no one knows it." [7] Princesses come in many different disguises.

So what about you? What mark will *you* leave in this world? How will you impact your school, your coworkers, your family and friends, the disadvantaged in your community, or the hungry children in some faraway country? How will *you* be a princess in disguise?

Do You Get It?

In the movie *Princess Diaries 2: Royal Engagement,* there's a scene in which Princess Mia is riding in a parade through the streets of Genovia. She spots some orphans in the crowd and orders that the carriage be stopped. She tells the orphans "to be a princess, you have to believe that you are a princess." She then orders a street vendor to give crowns to all the orphan girls and invites the orphans to walk with her in the parade. As one little orphan pulls her thumb out of her mouth and begins to tentatively wave at the crowd, Mia looks down at her and says, "Just remember—you *are* a princess."[8]

Remember our friend Sandee who so desperately wanted to be a beauty queen when she was a girl? After Sandee's heartbreaking and long period of rebellion, she eventually experienced a major transformation and returned to the God who gave her a purpose. She now uses the specific gifts and talents God's given her to make quilts that share God's message to a desperate world. And these aren't your granny's quilts! We're talking avant-garde, award-winning stuff here. For example, after seeing a television commercial where a young woman was proudly exclaiming, "I went from a size ten to a size two!" Sandee became furious with the public message that drives too many young girls on a destructive path of eating disorders and unhealthy body image. So she created these quilts:

© Sandee Winrow Milhouse. Used with permission.

© Sandee Winrow Milhouse. Used with permission.

Sandee is changing the world, one quilt at a time. In her own unique way, she's living out her calling. Sandee gets it.

What about you? Do you know you are a princess? Do you *really* know it? Acts 17:26 says, "From one man he made every nation of men, that they should inhabit the whole earth; and he determined the times set for them and the exact places where they should live." This means that God has put you here—at this time, where you are, at the exact moment you are reading these words—for a purpose.

So will you begin now to think of yourself as a warrior princess in disguise? Can you look in the mirror and see yourself as God made you—as a person of infinite worth? Can you look at your life as something meaningful, something amazing, something with a world-changing purpose?

Remember what Mia's grandmother said to her in the quote at the beginning of this chapter? "If you refuse to accept the throne, then the kingdom will cease to exist as we know it." Oh, sure, life will go on if you stop right here . . . if you decide you prefer the status quo over taking on the call of living as God's princess. Our kingdom will not cease to exist entirely . . . but it will not exist in the way that it could have if *you* had accepted the throne.

Status quo vs God's purpose!

Natural Princess

Get Your Shoes On!

Questions for Small Group Reflection

Read these questions and talk about them with your friends—or jot down your thoughts in your *One Girl Journal*.

1. How easy (or difficult) is it for you to believe that God calls you beautiful? What keeps you from believing that?

2. Do you act differently when you feel beautiful compared to times when you lack confidence? Share an example.

3. What's your gut reaction to the idea that you're a "princess in disguise"? Why? How might you approach tough situations differently if you thought of yourself as a princess in disguise?

4. Read Psalm 139. How does this psalm describe the way God feels about you and relates to you? How do the words and ideas in this psalm make you feel?

5. Do you believe that God has a purpose for your life? Why or why not?

2

what's my passion?

> "The place God calls you to
> is the place where your deep gladness
> and the world's deep hunger meet."
> —Frederick Buechner [1]

OK, you may be thinking, *I get it. I believe I'm here for a purpose. I believe God determined an exact time and place for me to be. I believe that he has plans for me . . . I just don't know exactly what those plans are. How do I figure it out?*

Oh, believe us, we understand. At a time when you're trying to figure out what to do after high school, which colleges to apply to, what to major in, and what career path to ultimately take, figuring out your whole life purpose can be a bit overwhelming. But we promise you this: If you resolve now to do the work to figure out what you're made of— what stirs your heart and what you're gifted to do—it'll make all the rest of your decisions easier.

Without a life mission, we can be tempted to run willy-nilly, getting involved in any project (no matter how worthwhile) that people ask us to—without considering whether it's truly the best use of our time and talents. The result is that we get burned out and our efforts are watered down. People without a clear sense of direction can end up spending years in the wrong career, feeling miserable and wondering what their life has been about. In fact we know a career counselor who told us that half of his clients are middle-aged people who are suffering from problems like tension, migraine headaches, and feelings of purposelessness—all because they did not figure out and stay true to their life's passion from an early age. Figuring out your own passion—your life mission—will take some time, but it's going to be well worth the effort.

Our friend Ellen knows all about the importance of starting early. She began to really zero in on her own life mission when she was just thirteen. "You have to start young if you want to be a leader," Ellen says. "You can't just wait for it to fall in your lap. You have to take control." She should know. When Ellen was in seventh grade, she went on her first inner-city mission trip. From there she's gone on to do short-term mission trips in Jamaica, Honduras, and Thailand. A passion to be involved in overseas missions has sparked in her heart.

Ellen's a shining example of 1 Timothy 4:12: "Don't let anyone look down on you because you are young, but set an example for the believers in speech, in life, in love, in faith and in purity." Ellen knows she serves the God who appointed an eight-year-old to the throne of Judah and, at the end of his reign, said of him: "Neither before nor after Josiah was there a king like him who turned to the LORD as he did—with all his heart and with all his soul and with all his strength, in accordance with all the Law of Moses" (2 Kings 23:25; see also 2 King 22:1, 2). Never, ever believe the lie that you are "too young" to make a difference, "too young" to lead the way, or "too young" to seek out God's plans for your future. In God's terms there's no such thing as "too young"!

And it's important that you do the work for yourself. Don't let other people determine your mission for you. Don't let circumstances, family, and friends (however well-meaning) cause you to drift into a life that you never intended. Ultimately you are the one who will be living your life, and you don't want to waste it by living out somebody else's dreams. Hang onto the dreams that are planted in your heart right now, and, relying on God, take charge of your own destiny!

Ellen tells us this was one of the hardest obstacles for her initially. Her parents, while very supportive and involved in overseas missions themselves, had the best intentions for her and wanted her to go to college first. It was really hard for Ellen to stand up and say that she was going to do something else, but she also didn't want to let her dreams slip by. She agreed with her parents that she needed to go to college, but she found a way to pursue her dream while taking college courses at the same time. After serving with Youth With A Mission in Canada, she's currently working full-time on her Bachelor's degree in social work. Wherever life takes her after school, we have no doubt that she'll continue to be a world changer.

Proverbs 29:18 says, "Where there is no vision, the people perish" (*KJV*). *The Message* says it this way: "If people can't see what God is doing, they stumble all over themselves; but when they attend to what he reveals, they are most blessed."

The dolphin pavilion at the Indianapolis Zoo is one of the coolest exhibits. You enter an enclosed underwater "bubble" and dolphins are swimming all around you—above, under, at you. It's amazing. The pavilion is so quiet that you get the sense that you are actually in the water with the dolphins. It's like you're in their world, quietly observing. One time we were visiting the zoo and were standing in the underwater dolphin pavilion. We were in utter awe, reflecting on God's marvelous creation, when we were suddenly distracted by a series of sounds. *Beep! Buzz! Ding!* We turned to look and saw a girl squatting on the ground, playing a hand-held computer game. She was so zeroed in on a dinky electronic game that she completely missed the magic going on all around her!

That little girl in the dolphin pavilion, missing it all, is the picture that comes to mind for us when we think about Proverbs 29:18 and someone *not* "attending to what he reveals." If we don't get intentional about looking at the big picture—about discovering our place on this planet—we risk the same thing. We'll end up getting distracted by the bells and whistles and missing out on God's amazing, phenomenal blessings.

So how do you start? How do you discover what *your* life mission is? That's what we're going to spend the rest of this chapter talking about.

Step 1: Get a Journal

As you figure out your life mission, you need a spot to scribble your thoughts, jot down your questions, write out your prayers, and doodle your dreams. If you don't already have one, get a copy of the *One Girl Journal* for yourself. (Or grab a simple spiral notebook and label it "My Big Dream" or whatever you want to call it.) You're going to use your *One Girl Journal* along your journey through this book to record all the work you're doing (with yourself, with God, with other people). Journaling through your thoughts and dreams will help you define your mission and how you're going to fulfill it. Writing your thoughts and prayers and questions will help tremendously in bringing central themes to the surface. It'll encourage you when you seem stuck in your plan. Research shows that we are more likely to accomplish goals that we write down. So get ready to do some writing with us!

The back part of your *One Girl Journal* is divided into 7 sections. If you're making your own journal, create some sections with these headings:

1. My Life Mission
This is a space for you to work through the questions and ideas we'll suggest in the following pages of this chapter. It's the spot where

you'll come up with a simple, focused, one-sentence mission statement for your life.

2. My Plan

This is where you'll start getting specific about the things you need to do to achieve your mission statement in this season of your life.

3. What's God Saying to Me?

This is where you'll record the insights God gives you in your prayer and devotional time with him, through uncanny circumstances, or what we call "divine appointments" with other people (more on that later!).

4. My Team

This is where you'll brainstorm a list of people who can help you realize your goal, organize your thoughts about their roles, and keep notes on your meetings with them.

5. My Progress

This is where you'll record your successes and make adjustments to your plan as needed.

6. Resources

As you begin to focus on your mission, you may be surprised by all the people you meet, books you hear about, or other opportunities to help you develop your skills and meet your goals. This is a spot where you can keep a running list of them.

7. Ideas

This is a good place to record any other random thoughts or action steps that pop into your mind that you want to follow up on as you continue on this amazing adventure.

Step 2: Get with God

While we call this step two, it's really the *first* priority—but we want you to have your journal ready so you can record your conversations with God. Psalm 37:4 says, "Delight yourself in the LORD and he will give you the desires of your heart." We used to think that this verse meant that if we pleased God, he would give us everything we wanted. But that doesn't quite jibe with the rest of the Bible. Now we've come to understand that it means if we delight in God above all else, wanting *him* more than his gifts, then he will put the desires in our heart that he intends for us to have. Those desires from God are part of his plan for us. Consider the words of Philippians 2:13: "For it is God who works in you to will and to act according to his good purpose." We aren't meant to float aimlessly through life. God has a plan for you, and if you turn to him, he will help you discover it. In his book *The Dream Giver,* author Bruce Wilkinson puts it this way:

> I've known people who can point to one conversation or spiritual experience when their future suddenly came into focus. But most of us don't see it all at once. We start with an inkling, a cluster of interests, a longing that won't go away. If we start there and set out, we give God a chance to show us more. One thing I know: God is not intentionally hiding your Dream from you. It's already in you. It's already *who you are.* Your opportunity is to discover it. [2]

Since God is the one who created you and your unique passions, the one who has determined the exact place and time and plan for you, the one who knows the good works he *already* prepared in advance for you, don't you think it might be a good idea to spend some time talking with him about his desires for you? Ask God to open your mind and heart to see his vision for your life.

Nineteen-year-old Lauren experienced God opening the eyes of her heart in a powerful way when she went on a mission trip to Nicaragua. In fact she says that the worship song "Open the Eyes of My Heart" became a theme song for her on that trip. She says, "He opened our eyes to things that broke our hearts, because we knew that his heart was breaking right along with ours." When Lauren started the trip, she was distracted from God and feeling spiritually disconnected. She was looking forward to being renewed and hearing from God on the trip, but she says, "He first had to persistently break down the walls—that I didn't even know existed—around my heart so it could look around with its newly opened eyes. It took nearly all week, but God perseveres and constantly goes after us. He kept at it until every brick of that wall was crumbled. Then he swept it clean with his unfailing love." Lauren had asked God to soften her heart to the things that break his . . . and he did. She sought God's vision for her life and then she watched for his response. She says, "I'm not really sure what God wants me to do next . . . but I do know that I don't want to ever ignore God again. And I definitely don't want to say no to whatever he has in store for me next."[3]

God can speak to you on a mission trip, like he did to Lauren, but he can also speak just as powerfully to you at home, in your bedroom, in the middle of your everyday life. You've just got to do what it takes to truly *listen*. When you first start out with this kind of listening, it may look to other people like you're doing a whole lot of nothing. It takes a lot of thought. A lot of prayer. A lot of time diving into God's Word. A lot of silence and solitude. And a lot of journaling. It can look a lot like daydreaming, actually. Silence and solitude are two of the toughest things to accomplish in our culture. You've got a busy schedule! Friends and family are clamoring for your time. Maybe you're juggling a part-time job and volunteering and volleyball practice and show choir competition this month and, oh-by-the-way, you've got to study for a major test on Friday. But you can't possibly prioritize all these things and move forward to the next step without ample quiet time with God. So determine that you'll spend a lot of time with him up front (like setting aside a whole Saturday morning) and commit to discipline yourself to spend some time with him every day too.

When you get with God, pour out your heart to him by writing your prayers in your journal. Start by telling him that you want to fulfill his purposes for your life, and ask him to guide you in your search and open the eyes of your heart so that you may see what he has in mind for you. Tell God you're willing to give up your *own* dreams and goals and ask God to replace those with *his* plans for your life. Invite him to lead you each step of the way as you try to figure out what his calling is in your life. Ask God to help you be obedient to him in following where he leads and seek his help in overcoming any obstacles along the way.

Step 3: Talk to Yourself

Your life mission is going to be something that you're very passionate about and that you're gifted by God to do. After all, if he has a plan for you're life, he's created you with the skills and passions and abilities to *do* that plan (with his help, of course!). So to find out what your mission is, you need to understand yourself very well. Start by thinking about and writing honest answers in your journal to the following questions:

What gives me energy?

You know that feeling you get when you love to do something so much that time flies by when you're doing it? When you could literally work on it all through the night and not get tired? That's how you know when you're in your groove—when you're working closely to your life mission. What kinds of discussions, ideas, or causes energize you?

What have I always wanted to be when I grow up?

Your knowledge of all the possibilities was more limited in elementary school, so think beyond whether you said nurse, or teacher, or ballerina. Think about what's *behind* those roles rather than those specific careers. For example if you always wanted to be a nurse, maybe it's because you're into caring for others hands-on. If you said teacher, perhaps you love learning and reformatting information so that it is easily digestible to others. If you said ballerina, perhaps you're a creative person who loves using artistic expression as a way to serve others.

If I won the lottery, what would I do with the money?

Many people respond with, "I'd quit work," or "I'd travel," or "I'd buy everything my family and I need and just sit back and enjoy it." But those things don't really fulfill us for the long-term—as we've already seen, we were created for a purpose! God made us each with a desire to *do* something! Assuming all your basic needs were met and you won the lottery, what would you do with the money?

What does a great day look like for me?

Margaret Thatcher, the first female prime minister in European history, said, "Look at a day when you are supremely satisfied at the end. It's not a day when you lounge around doing nothing; it's when you've had everything to do, and you've done it."[4] Not only is it a day when we've accomplished everything we've had to do, but a day in which those things we've had to do were also extremely satisfying. What would a day like that look like for you?

What causes do I really care about most?

You have to be *moved* by the idea. Is your heart in it? What about the world makes you angry? What makes you cry? What makes you pound the table, stand on your feet, and scream, "Something has to be done about this!"? Those are all pretty good clues that point you toward the things you care about most.

What groups of people do I really care about?

This may be the elderly or children or your peers or the homeless or certain cultural groups. Think about how you could match your skills and passions to meet the needs of the particular people group you really have a heart for.

What have I achieved so far in life? What am I really good at?

Make a list of all the things you've done so far that you're proud of. Did you work really hard to get on the basketball team? Are you proud of your ability to responsibly care for little kids? Did you set up a lemonade stand one summer to raise money for a cause? Did you join the student council and make changes at your school? Now what specifically did you contribute in those situations—was it organizational skills, the ability to inspire people, public speaking, writing, or managing a team? Try to get at the heart of what you enjoyed the most about your achievements and why.

Who do I admire most?

Your role models will give you a huge clue about the subject matters that you're most naturally drawn to. Maybe there's a certain teacher or coach that you especially enjoy hanging out with. Think about what it is about that person that draws you to them and how that might be a clue to your own passions.

What do I want to be most remembered for?

In his later years novelist Leo Tolstoy (who'd already written many great works of literature including *War and Peace*) was plagued with the question: "What meaning will my life have after I am dead?" It haunted him to the point of near suicide, so he set out to discover and do what was really most important. Pursuing that question drove him back to Jesus' teachings, and he came to this conclusion (in his book *Confession*): "'Live, seeking God, for there can be no life without God.' And more powerfully than ever a light shone within me and all around me, and this light has not abundoned me since."[5] Don't wait until you're fifty to start figuring it out! What are the most important things you would want people to know about what you did with your life?

What does my perfect life look like?

Imagine for a moment that your life would be perfect in five years. OK, what did you think of? What does "perfect" look like to you? Or how about in ten years? What kinds of things do you picture yourself doing?

What would I attempt if I knew I could not fail?

Time after time in the Bible, we witness God using unlikely characters to achieve miraculous results so that he gets the glory—so that the world will know who he is. So kick the barriers and roadblocks and potential failures out of your mind for a moment. C. S. Lewis wrote: "You thought you were going to be made into a decent little cottage: but He is building a palace. He intends to come and live in it Himself."[6] What would you dare to do that you know only God can accomplish for you and through you?

How do I think God might be using all of this to point me toward my life mission?

Look back on your answers to all of these questions. What patterns do you see coming to the surface? How might God be using all of it to clue you in on your life mission?

Step 4: Write Your Life Mission

Whew. If you've made it through Step 3, you've done a lot of work, girl! Give yourself a pat on the back. You've done more than most young women (more than most adults, for that matter) ever do in trying to figure out what it is they've been put on this earth to do! But if you're an overanalytical type like Kim, you can get stuck in Step 3. As a wise mentor once said to Kim, "You have to be OK with knowing that you will never have 100 percent of the information you need to make this decision—you're going to have to be OK with 80 percent."

So here goes: *write it down*. Laurie Beth Jones, in her book *The Path*, says that a good life mission statement should:

1. Be no more than a single sentence long

2. Be easily understood

3. Be something you're able to recite from memory [7]

It should also be wide open enough to encompass a lot of different jobs, causes, or activities for the long term. The specific jobs or projects that you're involved in will change over time, but your goal is to have them all connect with your broader life mission in some way. As Laurie Beth Jones says, "A personal mission statement acts as both a harness and a sword—harnessing you to what is true about your life, and cutting away all that is false." [8]

Your mission statement should include an **action**, a **core value**, and a **target cause** or group that you are most passionate about. For example . . .

My mission is to teach and motivate young women to realize their God-given potential.

My mission is to organize programs to help the homeless toward self-sufficiency.

My mission is to use my artistic abilities to create awareness and raise support for orphans in Africa.

My mission is to inspire a love of overseas missions in my community.

Are you starting to get the picture? Now it's your turn. Turn to page 138 in your *One Girl Journal* (or a blank page in your notebook) and write:

My mission is to _____ *for*
(what)

_____ .
(whom)

Fill in the blanks. Try writing it a few different ways. What feels best to you? Don't worry if it doesn't quite fit yet—this is just a starting point. Consider your statement a rough draft for now. You'll be surprised how the work we'll do in the next few chapters, along with the experiences you have as you go through these exercises and the conversations you have with God along the way, will start to come together to help you refine it. It may go through a few revisions before it's just right. The important thing is that you're getting serious about the role that is yours to play.

Step 5: Talk to Others

Once you have a draft of your life mission, share it with a few people you think are living out their own life mission, such as some close friends, your parents, your youth pastor, a trusted teacher, or a mentor. Ask them what they see in you. Ask them what things they think you're good at. Ask how they would tweak your mission statement based on what they know about you. While they don't yet know it, this is also an important first step to getting them on your team of supporters who will help you begin specific projects to fulfill your mission. Simply sharing your mission with others will also get them thinking about how they might help you reach it.

Your "One Thing"

In the movie *City Slickers,* three middle-aged urban guys decide to go off to a ranch and volunteer on a cattle drive as a way to work through their own personal crises. At one point the rough cowboy boss, Curly, says to Billy Crystal's character, Mitch Robbins, "Do you know what the secret of life is? . . . One thing. Just one thing." Curly tells Mitch to stick to that "one thing" and nothing else matters. Mitch asks, "But, what is the 'one thing'?" Curly mysteriously replies, "That's what *you* have to find out." [9]

"One thing" also happens to be a popular theme in the Bible. In Psalm 27:4 David says, "One thing I ask of the LORD, this is what I seek: that I may dwell in the house of the LORD all the days of my life, to gaze upon the beauty of the LORD and to seek him in his temple." And Jesus tells his friend Martha in Luke 10:41, 42: "You are worried and upset about many things, but only one thing is needed. Mary has chosen what is better, and it will not be taken away from her."

And remember when the teacher of the law came to Jesus and asked, "Of all the commandments, which is the most important?" Jesus answered, "The most important one . . . is this: 'Hear, O Israel, the Lord our God, the Lord is one. Love the Lord your God with all your heart and with all your soul and with all your mind and with all your strength.' The second is this: 'Love your neighbor as yourself.' There is no commandment greater than these" (Mark 12:28-31). In essence Jesus was saying that the *one thing*—the most important thing of all—is to love God with everything you have. The second is to love others. As Christians our personal mission must ultimately fulfill this overriding purpose: loving God and loving others. Exactly *how* you go about doing that will be unique, based on your own passions and gifts.

So what's your passion? Be honest—in your heart of hearts, you already know it. How does your mission enable you to love God and love others? Thomas à Kempis, a German monk who lived in the fifteenth century, urged Christians to "Use temporal things properly, but always desire what is eternal." [10] Or as we'd put it, set down the computer game . . . see the dolphins!

Get Your Shoes On!

Questions for Small Group Reflection

Read these questions and talk about them with your friends—or jot down your own thoughts in your *One Girl Journal*.

1. Have you ever thought about your life mission? Why or why not? Do you find the prospect of creating a life mission statement intimidating or inspiring?

2. What are your main passions and gifts? Describe them. (If you want, take turns telling each other what passions and gifts you see in one another. Either say them out loud or write them down and have one person read them out loud.)

3. Pick one of the "Step 3: Talk to Yourself" questions (on p. 38) and share your answer. How does the question help you discover more about yourself and who God is calling you to be?

4. Spend ten minutes of quiet time writing your own first draft of a mission statement. Remember, each mission statement should include an action, a core value, and a target cause or group that you are most passionate about.

My mission is to _____ for _____.
                          (what)   (whom)

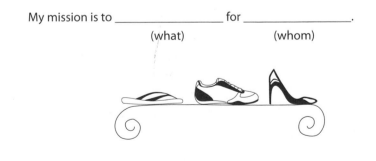

3

what kind of
leader am I?

> "There are different kinds of gifts, but the same Spirit.
> There are different kinds of service, but the same Lord.
> There are different kinds of working,
> but the same God works all of them in all men"
> (1 Corinthians 12:4-6).

Claudia: You can tell a lot about a girl by the way she eats a lollipop. Trust me—I am a lollipop expert. As a former teacher and youth minister, I've given away more lollipops than your local bank drive-through window. You could buy a small country with the money I've spent on lollipops! I've collected flavors like piña colada in Florida, peach in Georgia, and rocky road in the Great Smoky Mountains. I've had lollipops in the form of Raggedy Ann and Andy, Sponge Bob, all kinds of animals, and—my personal favorite—a pelican. Hard or soft, sweet or sour, with chocolate or bubble gum in the middle . . . I love them all. Yes, I'm a lollipop expert. And Kim and I can tell a lot about what kind of leader **you** are by the way you eat one. We call it Lollipop

*Leadership. In fact, if you have a lollipop somewhere nearby, go grab one and start eating it as you read this chapter. Pay attention to the way you're eating it and whether you see **yourself** in any of the following Lollipop Leader types . . .*

The Chomper

An old commercial for Tootsie Pops® featured a kid walking up to a turtle with a Tootsie Pop in hand. He asks the turtle how many licks it takes to get to the chocolate middle of the sucker, but the turtle doesn't know—he always ends up taking a bite to get to the middle! So the kid asks an owl the same question and the owl decides to try counting. Despite his best efforts to patiently lick, even the wise owl can't resist chomping into the sucker. The tagline of the commercial was: "How many licks does it take to get to the Tootsie Roll® center of a Tootsie Pop? *Crunch.* The world may never know."

The Chomper is the type of girl who will never know how many licks it takes to get to the center of a Tootsie Pop. She's the kind of person who grabs the first lollipop she touches in the jar, rips off the wrapper, and chomps into it, leaving a glob of hard candy stuck to her molars. She's a gutsy, get-it-done, roll-up-her-sleeves-and-dive-right-in kind of girl. She's a young woman who goes for it.

Jael (described in Judges 4:17-24) was a Chomper. God's people had been cruelly oppressed by the Canaanites for twenty years, but the time had come for God to liberate them. Deborah, a prophet and judge, was the key leader of God's people at the time. God spoke through Deborah and called his people to fight the mighty Canaanite army. Then Deborah said something really surprising: she said that God's people would have victory over the enemy through the actions of a woman (Judges 4:9). Jael was that woman.

Jael was minding her own business in her tent when Sisera, the commander of the enemy army, came by. She invited him into her tent and then gave him a drink and a place to rest. But when he fell asleep, she seized the opportunity to win the battle for her people: she killed Sisera with a tent peg. Jael took bold and courageous action, even when the task before her was gruesome and scary.

Seventeen-year-old Rita is a great example of a Chomper. On a family vacation to California, she was struck by the contrast between the wealthy elite she saw on a particular beach and the homeless and poor people begging at that very same beach. She saw people who had much more than they needed and she also saw people who carried all their worldly possessions in a backpack. Rita witnessed the homeless sleeping on the beach, begging for money, or digging through trash cans for pieces of leftover food. She was stirred by the fact that the two classes of people were not intermingling; Rita wondered how the extremely rich could walk right past people with such huge needs every day and not do anything about it.

So on their last vacation day, Rita's family ate a breakfast of donuts, bagels, and orange juice. When they were finished eating, they still had some food left over. Full of determination that even many of the local celebrities did not have, Rita took a short walk to the beach and offered the leftover pastries and juice to an obviously poor (if not homeless) woman sitting on a blanket with her young child. See, Rita just couldn't sit by and wait for someone else to help. She had to act. [1] Rita is a Chomper—someone who gets things done and has great potential to be a real world changer.

Are you a Chomper like Rita? Someone who takes action? Someone who's not afraid to just go for it? If you are, keep this caution in mind:

Chompers need to be careful of acting too impulsively without calculating the risks or falling into the trap of thinking they can do it alone. As Claudia's niece Ashley, a bona fide Chomper says, "Sometimes my mouth goes faster than my head." Proverbs 19:2 puts it this way: "Enthusiasm without knowledge is no good; haste makes mistakes" (*NLT*). Chompers also need to watch out for the temptation to follow their *own* plans without taking the time to truly seek God's guidance. If you're a Chomper, be sure to always take time to seek out God's will and make sure you've got people in your life who balance your ability to act quickly with their abilities to plan and consider the details.

Do these words describe you? If so, you might be a

Chomper.

☐ **Risk taker**—"I'm the first one to jump off the diving board."

☐ **Opinionated**—"I have important ideas that others need to hear."

☐ **Adventurous**—"I'd rather be bungee jumping than reading a book."

☐ **Resolute**—"It's better to ask for forgiveness than to beg for permission."

The Saver

The first dead giveaway of the Saver is how she unwraps a lollipop.

She'll open the lollipop slowly, taking great care not to tear the paper. She'll meticulously smooth out the wrapper and fold it evenly in half, then in half again. She'll take a few savored licks and then out comes the wrapper, which is unfolded and the lollipop is rewrapped and saved for later. The Saver is someone who's got a great ability to delay gratification and has a longer-term vision. She's a girl who can be very conservative and resourceful.

Abigail, described in 1 Samuel 25, was really resourceful, and we think she fits the Saver category. The Bible says she was beautiful and intelligent. She used her smarts to save her husband Nabal's life. He'd refused to give any food to David and his soldiers, so David wanted them to kill Nabal and his servants. When one of the servants ran to Abigail with the news, Scripture tells us that "Abigail lost no time" (1 Samuel 25:18). She loaded her donkeys up with a huge feast for David and his men.

As soon as Abigail saw David, she jumped off her donkey and fell at his feet, begging him to forgive her husband's offense. She persuaded David not to take revenge on her husband. After hearing her, David praised God and acknowledged that if it hadn't been for Abigail's good sense and quick action, he would have acted violently to avenge himself. Abigail's long-term vision and resourcefulness saved the day.

Kim: Tori is another Saver. I met Tori (then about ten years old) on a mission trip in Mexico. Tori's a girl who totally inspires me! For example, she once saw a television program requesting funds for an overseas mission pharmacy. Tori was so moved that she decided to save her tooth-fairy money and Christmas money to send to the pharmacy. When she sent invitations to her birthday party, she requested that her guests bring money for the pharmacy instead of bringing birthday gifts. Tori raised money any way she could think of. Though she was young, Tori was able to raise enough funds to support the pharmacy for an entire year!

Another time, Tori decided she wanted to collect shoes for the poor. She saved her old shoes and asked everyone she knew to save their old shoes too. They ended up with a garage full of boxes of shoes to donate to people in need! Any time friends went on a mission trip, Tori sent shoes along with them.

Tori was a quiet girl with an unassuming manner—but her resourcefulness ended up inspiring her entire family to go on a mission trip together. Since that trip they've gone on several more together! Young Tori has grown up a bit since I last saw her. She's now a preteen who leads a prayer group with nine other world-changing girls.

Are you a Saver like Abigail and Tori? If you are, then you've got great potential to use your resourcefulness to change the world. But be on the lookout for a potential downside of your leadership style. Jesus told a story in Matthew 25 about a servant whose master entrusted him with money. Rather than investing the money, the servant buried it to try to keep it safe; in the story the servant is chastised by his master. Like the man in the parable, a Saver may miss the boat by never quite taking action. She can get stuck in "analysis paralysis" and end up not doing *anything* with the gifts she's been given or the resources she's saved. If you're a Saver, be sure to get people on your team who can help you envision and act upon what you can *do* with what you've saved.

Do these words describe you? If so, you might be a

Saver.

☐ **Resourceful**—"I quickly spot ways to put my talent, time, and money—as well as the resources of others—to good use."

☐ **Conservative**—"It would be no big deal for me to give up Starbucks® coffee and instead donate the money to women in Africa who want to start their own businesses."

☐ **Long-term visionary**—"I often consider how my actions today pave the way for what I want to accomplish in the future."

☐ **Detail-oriented**—"When working on a team project, I'm the one who handles the details no one else wants to think about."

The Twirler

Think of the Twirler as a creative, head-in-the-clouds, free-spirit type of girl. She may run to the lollipop jar in hopes of finding a blue one for no other reason than to enjoy the thrill of having a blue-colored tongue! She'll open the lollipop, wad up the wrapper, and make a game of throwing it in the wastebasket. She'll pop the lollipop in her mouth and spin it wildly.

Twirlers have great imaginations and believe that anything is possible. They're dreamers with big ideas, and they don't let others discourage them. It's a joy to be around Twirlers because they're optimists and they remind us to have fun in life. Remember our friend Ellen from the previous chapter who'd started figuring out her life mission when she was just thirteen? Kim first met Ellen at church camp where she was a student leader. The first time they met, Ellen was wearing a T-shirt that read: "I can dance naked if I want to." On the back, it said, "2 Samuel 6:21-22." This passage describes a time in the Bible when David was dancing publicly (in his skivvies!) in celebration as the ark of the covenant was brought back to Jerusalem. Now Ellen's not *really* the type of girl who would dance naked—at least not in public! But her bold, attention-grabbing shirt is just one example of how she *is* an individual who isn't afraid to be the unique person God created her to be. Ellen's own interpretation of "dancing naked" has been to go to Thailand to serve tsunami victims, to befriend drug addicts in prison, and to deliver roses to prostitutes. She's a definite Twirler at heart.

We think Moses' sister Miriam was a Twirler too. She first showed her ability to believe the impossible when, as a young girl (scholars believe not even yet a teenager), she guarded the basket that was carrying baby Moses down the Nile River. At just the right moment, when Pharaoh's daughter found Moses and was going to take him to raise in the palace, Miriam jumped out of hiding and suggested that she could find a mother to nurse the baby until he was weaned and the princess could raise him. In doing so she guaranteed Moses' early connection to his Hebrew roots (Exodus 2:1-10).

Years later, when the Hebrew people were miraculously freed from slavery in Egypt, Miriam was by her brother Moses' side. She led the freed slaves in singing and dancing after the Red Sea had been parted and they'd crossed on dry land (Exodus 15:20, 21). One book about important women in the Bible describes her this way:

> She rallies the troops and keeps them focused as they
> leave Egypt—otherwise there would have been chaos,
> confusion, rioting, and looting. Almost like a lighthouse

that guides ships safely to shore through a treacherous fog, Miriam sings and directs the people to follow her brother Moses. Like Moses, Miriam gives guidance in time of need and demonstrates her faith and praise of God. [2]

A Twirler's strength comes in her ability to inspire. Twirlers encourage those of us with our feet on the ground that the impossible *can* be achieved.

Are you a Twirler like Ellen or Miriam? Are you somebody like Lucy in *The Chronicles of Narnia* who's not afraid to assert, "I'm telling you, there's another land inside the wardrobe!" Are you someone with big dreams who's excited to show the world who you are, quirks and all? If you are, keep an eye on this challenge that many Twirlers face. Though Twirlers are usually great at getting the ball rolling, they often don't like to get bogged down in details, and sometimes this means they end up dropping the ball entirely instead of following through on their projects and ideas. Twirlers need to surround themselves with people who can pay attention to details and who can transform their vision into reality.

Do these words describe you? If so, you might be a
Twirler.

☐ **Dreamer**—"My motto is: 'If you can dream it, you can achieve it.'"

☐ **Nonconformist**—"I like to stand out from the crowd."

☐ **Creative**—"So many ideas, so little time!"

☐ **Motivator**—"It's easy for me to sell my ideas and get people on my team."

The Strategist

You can spot the Strategist by the look of intense determination on her face. With furrowed brow, she nibbles on her pencil eraser as she considers the optimal way to distribute the lollipops based on survey findings. While eating her own lollipop, she rotates it about every twenty licks or so, to be sure to keep the surface evenly shaped. Sweat may break out on her forehead as she focuses on the task at hand. When she's finished she journals the results and begins to design a process (complete with flow charts) for future sucker Strategists. She's the kind of girl who arranges her bookshelf in alphabetical order, uses different colored highlighters for different classes, and makes to-do lists on a regular basis.

Everyone needs a Strategist on her team. Strategists are excellent planners. They're great at organization. They often have the ability to recognize others' talents and know exactly how to put others to work. The Bible highlights several women who were Strategists. There's Rahab (in Joshua chapters 2 and 6), who devised a plan to hide the Israelite spies until the coast was clear and negotiated for the protection of her family. There's Moses' mother, who strategized to keep her infant son alive, first by hiding him for three months and then by sending him in the basket down the Nile River rather than letting the Egyptians kill him (Exodus 2). And there's Naomi, who strategized a matchmaking plan for Ruth, who was noticed by Boaz (thanks to Naomi's suggestions), and who ultimately married him (check out the book of Ruth). As you can see, God uses Strategists to do important and amazing things!

Do you think you may be a Strategist like Rahab, Moses' mother, and Naomi? If you are, you need to be extra careful about one thing: Strategists can sometimes be . . . well . . . *manipulative*. The Bible shows us one of these examples too. In a scheme that would make *The Parent Trap* twins proud, Rebekah plotted a way for her favorite son, Jacob, to trick his father into giving him the birthright that was really meant for his brother Esau (Genesis 27). Can't you just see Rebekah intensely rolling that lollipop around in her mouth as she stirred the stew, planning out the details of covering Jacob with animal skins so he would feel and smell like Isaac's favorite son, Esau? Rebekah's plan worked, but she and her son were deceitful in the process.

Of course, not all Strategists are manipulative. Strategists have great leadership potential. Take Macy, for instance—a teenage girl who's been a leader at the camp we run. Macy has a knack for taking our vision of what we want the campers to learn and breaking it down into measurable steps. On her own initiative, she'll devise a poster-board-size chart with daily goals for the girls in her group and a reward system for meeting those goals. Rather than coming across as a taskmaster, the campers in her group love the structure and encouraging environment Macy creates. In fact, in her first summer as a student leader, her peers voted her as "Most Valuable Rookie"! Macy's a great example of someone who uses her natural inclinations to plan and strategize for God's glory . . . and lives get changed in the process.

Strategists are very driven and see the big picture, yet they have a wonderful ability to also understand the small, individual parts that make up that big picture. They know what it will take to accomplish the goal. They may not have all of the skills themselves, but they know what kind of people they need on their team. If you're a Strategist, embrace it! You've been given a wonderful gift. But learn from Rebekah's example too, and always be careful to keep your motives in check.

Do these words describe you? If so, you might be a
Strategist.

☐ **Goal-oriented**—"I know what I want to achieve and what it will take to get there."

☐ **Decisive**—"I make a plan and stick to it."

☐ **Problem Solver**—"I enjoy the challenge of figuring out how to get from Point A to Point B."

☐ **Organized**—"I live my life by my to-do list."

The Optimist

The Optimist is the kind of girl who always sees the lollipop jar half full. When you ask her which is her favorite flavor, her response is likely to be, "I love them all!" She savors every taste. When black licorice is the only flavor left, she says, "That's great! I've never tried black licorice before, and today I get to experience something new!"

The ultimate story of an Optimist that we've ever heard was from Corrie ten Boom, a Nazi concentration camp survivor who told her story in an autobiography called *The Hiding Place.* Corrie and her sister Betsie had been taken to the Ravensbruck concentration camp. They were packed into barracks with about 1,400 women, though the room was only built for about 400. They were forced to sleep on dusty, flea-infested straw mattresses. They were forced to work by loading heavy sheets of steel onto carts and given meals consisting of only one potato and a thin soup at lunch and a little turnip soup with a piece of black bread at night. They were often beaten, and the women who became too sick to work were sent to the gas chamber. Crammed in such close quarters, the women understandably began to complain and argue with each other.

Corrie tells the story of complaining about the fleas. She was taken aback when her sister Betsie, whom she credits with keeping the women's spirits up and constantly praying for peace among them, told her that God says in his Word that we are to give thanks in all circumstances. Betsie was even giving thanks to God in a prayer for the fleas! As they later discovered, the fleas were *exactly* what kept the Nazi guards from coming into their barracks and harassing them. The fleas allowed them to have private time to pray and read the Bible (which Corrie had miraculously been able to smuggle in).[3] Wow . . . can you imagine having the hope and optimism of Betsie ten Boom? What an inspiring example. Whenever you're feeling discouraged by hard circumstances, try to remember Betsie and thank God for the "fleas"!

Hannah, even in the midst of deep personal grief, was an Optimist. In 1 Samuel 1, we read about Hannah's life; she was married to Elkanah, and he also had another wife named Peninnah. Peninnah had children, but Hannah didn't, and this was really hard for Hannah—she lived in a time and culture in which having children was a woman's main "job," so if you didn't have kids, you were viewed as a failure. To make matters worse, she had to endure hurtful criticism from Peninnah. Hannah was so upset that she wept and wouldn't eat. One time Hannah could no longer take it, and she stood up at the temple, crying bitterly, and prayed, "O LORD Almighty, if you will only look upon your servant's misery and remember me, and not forget your servant but give her a son, then I will give him to the LORD for all the days of his life" (1 Samuel 1:11). The priest Eli told her, "Go in peace, and may the God of Israel grant you what you have asked of him" (1:17). The next verse tells us that Hannah then finally ate something and that "her face was no longer downcast"

(1:18). She believed God—she was optimistic—in the face of a seemingly impossible situation! (Eventually God blessed Hannah with a son she named Samuel.)

We like to be around Optimists. Optimists keep us going when the going seems to get tough. They fill us with inspiration and hope. It's been said that optimism is what makes the teakettle sing, even when it's up to its neck in hot water! Are you an Optimist? If you are, remember to stay strong in the face of adversity . . . the rest of us need you! But be careful too of this potential hazard: sometimes Optimists have a hard time looking honestly at the potential downfalls of a situation. You need others in your life who will help you see the tough situations realistically so that problems can be dealt with.

Do these words describe you? If so, you might be an

Optimist.

☐ **Positive**—"I see the glass half full most of the time."

☐ **Cheerleader**—"I tend to be the one to encourage and rally the troops."

☐ **Social**—"I meet people easily and am very comfortable in large groups."

☐ **Idealist**—"I agree with Albert Einstein that 'imagination is more important than knowledge.'"[4]

The Critic

The Critic looks at the lollipop jar and immediately notices the flaws (such as a favorite flavor that's missing) or points out that the jar's getting a little empty and needs to be refilled. She's a girl who tends to be a perfectionist and can point out right away what's wrong with any given situation.

Martha, the sister of Lazarus and Mary, was a bit of a Critic. Remember when Jesus visited her home? Martha was in the kitchen being a good Martha Stewart (perhaps decorating with hand-made olive branch wreaths and baking a three-tiered fig cake with toasted almond slivers), while her sister Mary was sitting at Jesus' feet listening to his teachings. Martha went to Jesus and said, "Lord, don't you care that my sister has left me to do the work by myself? Tell her to help me!" (Luke 10:40). Ooh! Can't you just hear the whine in her voice? Can't you just see her fuming and thinking, *It's not fair!*?

John 11:5 tells us that Jesus loved Martha—in fact, she was one of Jesus' very close friends. So we can be sure it was with compassion that he replied, "Martha, Martha, . . . you are worried and upset about many things, but only one thing is needed. Mary has chosen what is better, and it will not be taken away from her" (Luke 10:41). We probably would not have been so gentle! We would have just said, "Get over it!"

Sometimes Critics have hurtful motives and their critiques can feel painful, especially if they're directed at you! When someone says disparaging things about you, always ask, "What lies beneath her words?" Is there anything truthful about what she's saying? Is there something you are responsible for? If so, go make amends. But if you've thought it over and don't honestly see any truth in a Critic's accusations, shrug it off. We would all do well to recognize the insights and truths well-meaning Critics bring up. While they may not always be communicated diplomatically, they can be valid.

So before we give Critics *too bad* of a rap, it's important to remember that Critics are important voices in our world. After all, what would we do without good movie critics who point out the very best films and help us avoid the duds? Or what about those friends we call on to critique our research papers, showing us how we can improve them before we turn them in? Being a Critic takes both guts and vision. Critics can point out potential pitfalls that others need to consider before embarking on a mission.

Critics are girls who aren't afraid to call a spade a spade. We can see this in Martha in another encounter she had with Jesus. In John 11:21, Martha saw Jesus after her brother Lazarus died. Rather than hiding her feelings, she honestly confronted Jesus about not coming sooner: "Lord, . . . if you had been here, my brother would not have died." But rather than reprimand her for questioning him, Jesus promised to bring Martha's brother back to life. Martha responded with great faith, saying, "I believe that you are the Christ, the Son of God, who was to come into the world" (John 11:27). She was able to see Jesus for who he really was—even when many of his disciples didn't yet understand Jesus' true identity! This encounter shows us that the bold honesty of a Critic, when tempered with true faith and deep humility, can be a powerful force of truth in the world.

So if you tend to be a Critic, realize that God gave you a particular ability to notice real details that need to be addressed, and he made you with a willingness to point out problems that others may overlook. But keep a *close* reign on your motives and your delivery style. Learn how to soften your criticisms so that they can be heard by others rather than hurting or discouraging them. When you consider others' feelings in the way you deliver your critiques and insights, they'll be better able to receive your suggestions with open hearts and open minds.

The Hider

Unfortunately many of us who may have been a Chomper or a Twirler at a younger age become a Hider when we hit the teen years and adulthood. As the name implies, a Hider doesn't like to be seen eating her lollipop. She's "too mature" for such childish antics. She still *secretly* enjoys eating lollipops, but, due to insecurities or the pressure to fit in, she'll pull the lollipop top off the stick and throw the stick away so no one will know what she's eating.

Being a Hider in leadership is like the song "This Little Light of Mine"—you're hiding your light under a bushel. Mia in *The Princess Diaries* was *initially* a Hider. At first she didn't want to be a princess. She liked her ordinary life just fine, thank you very much. Check out this conversation Mia had with her grandmother in the book:

> Then Grandmère sat down in the foofy chair next to mine and said, "Are you telling me you have no wish to assume

your rightful place on the throne?"

Boy, was I tired. "Grandmère, you know as well as I do that I'm not princess material, okay? So why are we even wasting our time?"

Grandmère looked at me out of her twin tattoos of eyeliner. I could tell she wanted to kill me but probably couldn't figure out how to do it without getting blood on the pink carpet.

"You are the heir to the crown of Genovia," she said in this totally serious voice. "And you will take my son's place on the throne when he dies. This is how it is. There is no other way."

Oh, boy.

So I kind of went, "Yeah, whatever, Grandmère. Look, I got a lot of homework. Is this princess thing going to take long?"[5]

Queen Esther in the Bible was initially a Hider too. In the fifth century BC, she was a Jewish girl living in Persia who had been chosen to become the wife of the king, Xerxes. At first her very life depended on being a Hider—she kept her Jewish ethnicity and beliefs a secret from the king for her own safety. Her cousin Mordecai heard that Haman, one of the king's top advisers, had a plan to destroy all the Jews in the kingdom. So Mordecai sent messengers to Esther, urging her to beg the king to save her people. In essence, she sent back the reply, "Are you crazy? Everyone knows that you don't go to the king in his inner court without being summoned! If I even try, unless the king shows me mercy by extending his golden scepter, I'll be killed! Besides, I haven't even *seen* the king in thirty days."

Esther was her people's only hope, but she was letting fear hide her calling. So Mordecai sent a message back to Esther that went something like this: "Do you think that just because you're in the palace, you're the only Jew who will be spared? If you keep silent now (if you continue to hide your lollipop!), you and your father's family will die." And then, in that now famous question that turned Esther from a Hider into a national hero, Mordecai asked her, "And who knows but that you have come to royal position for such a time as this?" (Esther 4:14; read the book of Esther for the whole story!).

If you've been given leadership abilities, no matter what your leadership style, you're meant to use them! Don't hide your talents because you're afraid of what others will think! And remember, there's a big difference between being *humble* (good!) and a *Hider* (not so good!). There are times when we leaders do need to downplay our gifts as we wait for the right timing or as we let others take the lead. It's important for Lollipop Leaders to be diplomatic and to admit when we need others' help. But that's a totally different scenario from hiding one's talents and abilities in order to not rock the boat. So if you think you might be a Hider, take some time right now to ask God to help you stop hiding away your leadership abilities.

Do these words describe you? If so, you might be a

Hider.

☐ **Super Analytical**—"One can never have enough information before acting."

☐ **Overly Cautious**—"What often prevents me from leading is a fear of failure."

☐ **Insecure**—"I have ideas and goals, but I'm afraid of what others will think."

☐ **Camouflaged**—"I prefer situations where no one notices me . . . where I just blend right in with the crowd."

We're One Big Bag of Assorted Flavors

Are you getting the idea? There are as many leadership types as there are ways to eat a lollipop. When we share this idea of Lollipop Leadership with teenagers, they often surprise us with all sorts of leadership types we hadn't yet considered. There's the Lollipop Giver (who buys suckers in bulk and is quick to share), there is the Invitational Lollipop Eater (who wants to shout the Lollipop Gospel from the mountaintops: "Hey! Here's a new bag of lollipops! Come and get 'em!"), and the Lollipop Mentor (who, with anticipation all over her face, brings a young lollipop protégé to the jar for the first time, shows her how to gently remove the lid and select the right flavor, and models every step from how to unwrap the paper to how to properly say "thank you").

There are two points we want you to get from reading through all these Lollipop Leadership styles. First, we want you to recognize who you are—both your strengths and your weaknesses. And of course you're more complex than just one simple label, even if one of the lollipop styles we described seems most dominant in your personality. God made you the way you are for a reason, and he intends to use *your* particular style to accomplish his will. So embrace who you are and learn to compensate for your weaknesses. As Mrs. Whatsit says in *A Wrinkle in Time,* "But of course we can't take any credit for our talents. It's how we use them that counts."[6]

Second, we want you to be able to recognize and appreciate the differences in others. When you step up to the plate to lead, you'll likely find yourself working with others who are not exactly like you. These differences are *good* things—but they can lead to challenges too. As girls, we tend to judge others, don't we? We assume we know the right way to eat a lollipop, and we tend to want to only hang out with people who eat lollipops the way we do. So when tensions crop up in your relationships, remember these Lollipop Leadership styles to offer yourself a little comic relief. It will enable you to laugh at your differences and say, "Oh, that's right—you're a Twirler." Or, "That makes sense—she's *such* a Chomper."

John the Baptist, the one chosen by God to pave the way for the Messiah, lived in the wilderness, wore clothes made of camel's hair, and ate wild locusts and honey. To say he lived on the fringe of society is a major understatement! Rahab was a prostitute who turned her life around, saved the Hebrew spies in Canaan, and ended up in Jesus' family tree. Mary of Magdala had once been possessed by demons, yet Jesus appeared to her *first* after his resurrection from the dead and sent her to go tell the others that he was alive. The point is this: God uses *all sorts* of unique individuals to change the world.

Now go grab a lollipop and savor his sweet love for you!

Get Your Shoes On!

Questions for Small Group Reflection

Read these questions and talk about them with your friends—or jot down your own thoughts in your *One Girl Journal*.

1. Grab a lollipop (or pass around a bag in your group) and start eating it. As you do, answer this question: Which type of Lollipop Leadership do you most identify with? Chomper, Saver, Twirler, Strategist, Optimist, Critic, or Hider? Why?

2. Can you think of other Lollipop Leader types that aren't mentioned in this chapter? Share some ideas you've got.

3. Now think about your family members or best friends. What are their Lollipop Leadership types? How can you improve the way you interact with them based on what you've read about their leadership styles?

4. People often tend to form their own little groups of friends just like them—and criticize those who are different. Why do you think it's like that? What examples of this have you seen?

5. How do you respond to the idea that "we're one big bag of assorted flavors"? How might God want you to do a better job of understanding and accepting people with different personalities and leadership styles? Share a specific example.

part 2

Do I Know Where I'm Going?

"You have brains in your head.
You have feet in your shoes.
You can steer yourself any direction you choose."
—Dr. Seuss, from *Oh, the Places You'll Go!* [1]

4

listen...

> "Whether you turn to the right or to the left,
> your ears will hear a voice behind you,
> saying, 'This is the way; walk in it'"
> (Isaiah 30:21).

This year at the camp we hold for girls, we asked two of the teen leaders, Kara (a Chomper) and Sylva (a Twirler), to teach the campers about how important it is for a world changer to be able to hear God's voice. In interview fashion Kara asked, "So, Sylva, exactly how *can* a girl tell when God's speaking to her?"

Always the actress, Sylva pressed her hands in the air and exclaimed wildly, "OK. It's like this: I am *so* in love with Orlando Bloom!" (Right away she got the attention of several giggly young campers infatuated with Orlando Bloom.) Sylva twirled her hair and went on: "I've seen all his movies! I buy every magazine he's in. I mean, he's got, like, the most *gorgeous* green eyes, you know?"

Sylva continued, dreamlike, "Anyway, one day I was sitting in the woods thinking about Orlando Bloom, and—all of a sudden—a *leaf* fell from a tree and landed right at my feet . . . and the leaf was *green*—the same shade as Orlando Bloom's eyes!"

Kara, looking confused, interrupted: "Wait a minute. What does *that* have to do with hearing from God?"

Sylva let out an exasperated huff and rolled her eyes: "Hello! It was like a *sign!* God was telling me I'm going to *marry* Orlando Bloom!"

Their example drew laughter from the crowd because we knew it was absurd, and yet probably not far from the claims that most of us have heard at one time or another. Have you ever heard someone claim to have gotten a sign from God or heard something from him? How do you react when someone approaches you with the words: "God told me . . ."? To tell you the truth, our first instinct when we hear those words is usually to be skeptical. We bristle because we know that people will often use "God told me" to justify all sorts of selfish things. People are sometimes so desperate that they'll use the most common of events—like a leaf falling from a tree—to back up their personal motives.

But we've both had experiences when we've *been* that person trying to convince someone that God has communicated something to us. There have been defining moments in our lives when we knew that we knew that we *knew* God had spoken to us. The truth is that God *does* speak to his people. We know from the Bible that God spoke to many people in both the Old Testament and New Testament. In one such instance, the angel of the Lord spoke to Hagar after she fled to the desert to escape Sarai's mistreatment. The angel told her that she was pregnant with a son and that she was to name him *Ishmael* (which means "God hears"). Hagar's response was, "You are the God who sees me . . . I have seen the One who sees me" (Genesis 16:13). She was so convinced of her own personal encounter with God that she called God the name *El Roi,* which means "the Living One who sees me." This passage gives us two really important clues about the character of God: God hears us, and God sees us.

In the fifteenth century, at only twelve years old, Joan of Arc claimed that she heard the voice of God telling her that she would save France from England. Although it was unheard of at that time for a woman to fight in battle, and in spite of her father's threats to kill her if she ever disgraced the family in such a way, she did in fact end up leading thousands of soldiers in many victories. While trying to recapture Paris, she was caught by English soldiers and, at age nineteen, was burned at the stake for her belief that God spoke to her.

Women in the Bible, like Hagar, and in church history, like Joan, have heard the voice of God. So what about us today? Doesn't it stand to reason that if we're going to change the world, we might want to spend a little time figuring out whether it's possible to still hear God's voice and, if so, *how?*

Not Alone

In the Old Testament God appeared in many forms—as a burning bush to Moses, as a pillar of cloud by day and a pillar of fire by night for the Israelites escaping Egypt, and over the ark of the covenant in the Holy of Holies in the temple. He gave Moses the law, and he spoke to his people through the prophets. Later the New Testament believers saw God in the flesh: Jesus.

Jesus hung out with them in their neighborhoods, he went fishing with them, he worshiped with them, he had fun with them . . . he talked directly with them. But at the very end of his time on earth, he presented them with a paradox. Right before he returned to Heaven, he said, "Surely I am with you always, to the very end of the age" (Matthew 28:20). On one hand, he was telling them he had to go away; on the other, he said he'd never leave them. So which was it?

Our answer is in the same explanation he gave his confused friends over two thousand years ago: "I tell you the truth: It is for your good that I am going away. Unless I go away, the Counselor will not come to you; but if I go, I will send him to you . . . [W]hen he, the Spirit of truth, comes, he will guide you into all truth" (John 16:7, 13). God speaks to us today, but not through burning bushes or pillars of cloud (at least *we've* never had that experience!). He speaks to us through the Holy Spirit living within us. When Jesus returned to Heaven, he didn't leave us, his people, alone! In fact, we're never alone . . . God's Spirit is always with us, to guide us and to help us understand God.

The Holy Spirit also helps us to talk *to* God. Romans 8:26, 27 says, "In the same way, the Spirit helps us in our weakness. We do not know what we ought to pray for, but the Spirit himself intercedes for us with groans that words cannot express. And he who searches our hearts knows the mind of the Spirit, because the Spirit intercedes for the saints in accordance with God's will." Have you ever been on your knees in prayer, so distressed about a situation you were praying about that you didn't even know what to say? According to this passage, the Holy Spirit communicates on our behalf in those times.

Or have you ever had a strong feeling that you should pray for someone, but you didn't know why? That's the Holy Spirit. One day over lunch, Kim asked her therapist friend, "Has God ever actually woken you up in the middle of the night to pray for someone?" Her friend smiled and nodded and told her story. She once woke up with the sense that she was to pray for a client that she hadn't heard from in years. Some time later she ran into that same woman in the grocery checkout lane. She asked her how she was doing and relayed the story of praying for her. The former client smiled and said, "I'm glad you did. It was at about that time that I was considering suicide." Now *that's* the Holy Spirit!

A Treasure

The Holy Spirit also acts as an interpreter, helping us to discern what God's saying to us through his other communication tools. And the primary tool he uses is the Word he's already given us: the Bible. Do you *know* what a treasure he has given us in the Bible? Don't take our word for it—listen to what the Bible says about itself:

- "For the word of God is living and active. Sharper than any double-edged sword, it penetrates even to dividing soul and spirit, joints and marrow; it judges the thoughts and attitudes of the heart" (Hebrews 4:12).

- "All Scripture is God-breathed and is useful for teaching, rebuking, correcting and training in righteousness, so that the man of God may be thoroughly equipped for every good work" (2 Timothy 3:16, 17).

- "Your word is a lamp to my feet and a light for my path" (Psalm 119:105).

Scripture is alive! It's relevant to us. It judges the attitudes of our hearts. It's inspired by God. It's a training manual to equip us for good works. It's at work in us. It's a light for our path. It was written by forty authors from different walks of life, in three different languages, over fifteen thousand years, on multiple continents, yet it reads as if written by one voice (God!). It's amazingly consistent and historically accurate. It's incredibly detailed in its prophecies and provides a pattern for things yet to come. It has practical truth for all the issues in your life. And it's exciting, with accounts of war, scandals, intrigue, and of course romance!

The Bible is about a God who loves you and pursues you and has something to say directly to *you*. Do you know what a treasure you have in it?! Old Testament believers didn't have the complete Scriptures, and New Testament believers copied the letters from the apostles and shared them among the churches and read them over and over for encouragement. Throughout history Christians faced execution for holding a copy of the Scripture in their own hands. People in some parts of the world today are still beaten, imprisoned, and sometimes killed if found with a copy of the Bible in their possession. Why? Because it is no ordinary book. It is the *mind of God*. It is *life* for us.

The Psalmist wrote: "I have hidden your word in my heart that I might not sin against you" (Psalm 119:11). When you read God's Word, meditate on it, and memorize it, you hide it in your heart. With God's Word stored up in your heart, God will bring stories and verses and truth back to mind for you in the most surprising ways and in unexpected moments. And at those times you'll know that you *know* that you have heard from God.

Cool Tools

OK, so here's the cool thing about God—He can talk to us any way he wants to! Besides his Word, God uses creation, experiences, and godly people to get his message through to us. A word of caution though: the Bible is *always* the last word. Romans 12:2 cautions us to "test and approve what God's will is—his good, pleasing and perfect will" through the renewing of our minds. In other words, we can't assume a falling green leaf is a sign from God! We should always come back to what God's Word says as our ultimate guide for us. If an experience you have or a message you hear from another person does not match up with what you know from Scripture, it cannot be true. God won't ever contradict what he's already told us in his Word. OK, with that said, let's explore some of the other cool communication tools God uses to speak to us today.

Creation

One of the things we love most about God is that he knows each of us intimately. He knows how to talk to us in a way that gets our attention . . . and he knows how to talk to *you* to get *your* attention. We mentioned in the first chapter that both of us are nature freaks (some would say freaks of nature!). Each of us has our own spiritual pathways—ways we best hear from God—and nature just happens to be it for us. We both feel like we hear from God best when we're hiking in the woods, fishing, or praying from a deer stand. So if you're having trouble hearing from God, could we just suggest a hike outdoors to clear your mind and to get alone with him? He might have something to say to you out there.

Kim: Not long ago I was studying the life of Joseph. I was feeling rejected, and the part where Joseph had been forgotten by the cupbearer and had to stay in prison for two more years really struck a chord with me. The Bible study guide I was using pointed me to Isaiah 49:15 where God tells his people, "Can a mother forget the baby at her breast and have no compassion on the child she has borne? Though she may forget, I will not forget you!" The writer of the study pointed out that although **people** may forget us and let us down, God will **never** forget us.

Sitting on the couch in front of my picture window that morning, I poured out my feelings to God. I cried and cried, and I told God that I felt like he'd forgotten me.

After I expressed all my feelings, I got up to refill my coffee. Walking back to the couch, something outside the picture window caught my eye. A closer look revealed that on the tree right outside my living room window there was an amazingly beautiful red-headed woodpecker. I stared at it a bit, and then I said out loud, "God! You're so cool! Good job!"

Then my eyes were drawn upward . . . and there was another, identical woodpecker! By this point I was going, "God! Two?! **Thank you!** That's **awesome!**"

But God wasn't done showing off. Further still, higher up on the tree trunk, was a **third** woodpecker!

In my heart I just knew this was God's way of saying, "Oh, it gets better! You think you want this thing, but—I am telling you—you're setting your sights too low! You're happy with one woodpecker? I've got **three!** Keep looking up! I have **way** more I want to give you!" Ephesians 3:20 immediately came to my mind, which describes God as "him who is able to do immeasurably more than all we ask or imagine, according to his power that is at work within us." And I just enjoyed God in that moment and relished the comfort of his love for me and his desire to bless us with wonderful gifts.

The Bible tells us that God communicates through his creation: "Since the creation of the world God's invisible qualities—his eternal power and divine nature—have been clearly seen, *being understood from what has been made,* so that men are without excuse" (Romans 1:20, italics added). Psalm 19:1 puts the same idea this way: "The heavens declare the glory of God; the skies proclaim the work of his hands." What about you? Have you ever had an experience in which God spoke to you through his creation? Maybe you were awestruck by a two-thousand-pound bison on a mountainside or by the detail in a monarch butterfly's wings. Maybe a cool breeze gave you a sense of peace and reminded you to stop and smell the roses. Or have you ever thrown a blanket down in your backyard at night and gazed up at the stars and just pondered the mystery of gravity?

You may be into nature like us—but even if you *aren't*, God can still speak to you through the amazing world he's made. Keep your eyes peeled and your ears open . . . you may be surprised by what God shows you today.

Experiences

God can also speak to you through the circumstances and experiences in your life. Here's just one story (we've got tons!) of a time God communicated to Claudia this way . . .

(Claudia: One day I was heading to work, and I felt like I'd really blown it the day before. I'd actually avoided a woman I saw come into the church who I knew needed a listening ear, I'd snapped at my husband, I'd listened to gossip, and I felt like I should have prepared more for a Bible lesson I'd given. I felt really, really down—like a total failure. As I drove, I talked to God: "I am so inadequate for this job . . . I don't know why you put me here . . . I feel so stupid."

At this point on my drive, like a shining beacon of hope, I saw a Starbucks coffeehouse sign. I pulled up to the drive-through and said, "I need a **venti** café mocha with all the fat and whipped cream you've got." I drove up to the window, scrambling in my purse for the money. As the barista handed me the coffee, he said, "Don't worry about it—it's already paid for."

I looked at the car in front of me then glanced inside the store, looking for a friend who must have seen me and done this favor. I didn't see anyone I recognized. The barista said again, "Don't worry about it—it's already paid for."

The phrase rang in my ears all the way to the church where I work. "It's been paid for." And it sunk in. I knew that I **knew** God was telling me that the work for all my inadequacies has already been done. My sins have already been paid for—on the cross—and my job is simply to stay connected to Jesus so that I can lead others to him.

I never found out who paid for my coffee, but I do know who was behind it all. So I walked into my office with a light heart, thanking God for the coffee.

God doesn't always speak through circumstances in such dramatic ways—sometimes it's in the little things, like seeing a smile from a stranger that reminds you to hope in God, getting a job that gives you a chance to earn the money you need for a mission trip, or receiving a very specific answer to a very specific prayer.

Godly People

God often uses other people to communicate with us. The advice of godly friends can show us God's wisdom. Their well-timed words of encouragement can lift us up when we're down. And sometimes God uses others to point out big problems in our lives and to show us where we need to get back on track.

Kim: God once spoke to me in a really direct way through our friend Ellen. She'd been part of our girls' camp that summer; Ellen taught the girls about missions in Uganda and the hardships faced by the Ugandan people. Each morning after Ellen spoke, we'd pass coffee cans to collect the spare change the campers wanted to donate to Ellen's upcoming trip to Uganda.

OK, now fast-forward a few months. I was feeling sorry for myself about something and talking to God about my feelings. I prayed honestly, telling him that in my head, I know he's good, but I really needed to know and feel it in my **heart** too. "Are you good, God?" I prayed, "Can I really trust you with my concerns?"

The next morning, realizing it was the day Ellen was leaving for Uganda, I said a prayer for her. Later that evening, as I was pulling out of my driveway, I picked up the mail from my mailbox. Driving down the highway, the harvest moon was right at my eye level—unbelievably **big** and orange and following me as I drove. Keeping my left hand on the steering wheel, I used my right hand to thumb through the mail in the seat beside me. I spotted a personal card and tore into it first. It was from Ellen; she wrote, "Did I ever tell you that the amount of money I raised at camp was exactly what I asked God for?"

Her next words blew me away: "He **is** a good God." And in that moment I knew that I **knew** that God had used Ellen, had caused her card to arrive not coincidentally on the very morning after I'd asked him, "Are you good?" I started bawling my eyes out; driving down the highway, with that bigger-than-life orange moon shining bright. "Yes, Ellen," I said through my tears and with a smile, "He **is** a good God!"

So How Do We Hear from God?

Ever known one of those strong, silent guys? Maybe it's your brother or one of your friends from youth group? Conversations with them can feel like pulling teeth, sort of like . . .

"How's it going?"

"Fine."

"What's new?"

"Nothing."

"How's soccer going?"

"Fine."

"What did you do today?"

"Nothing."

But then a guy like this gets a girlfriend and . . . wow! Some magic occurs in his brain, and he suddenly begins spending hours talking to her on the phone (and texting her in between phone calls), telling stories, sharing dreams, opening up, talking about anything and everything . . . and nothing at all. Why? Because it's *worth it* to him to invest the time in really getting to know his new girlfriend.

Isn't that what we all tend to do when we have a crush on someone? We clear our schedules to spend time with him. We check our cell phones every few minutes for missed calls. We take time to study him and what he likes—whether it's sports or war history or video games or whatever else it is that boys are into. That's the kind of devotion God wants from you—to know you just want to spend time with him for nothing other than to get to know him better. He wants intimacy with you. So, how do you develop intimacy with God?

Be Still

To develop intimacy with anyone, including God, we must "unplug" from our iPods, our cell phones, our instant messaging, and devote time alone with him. We must develop the same attitude David had toward his relationship with God in Psalm 42:1, 2:

> As the deer pants for streams of water,
> so my soul pants for you, O God.
> My soul thirsts for God, for the living God.
> When can I go and meet with God?

When Kim was little, she cherished time alone with her dad. He worked long hours, and evenings were hectic with dinner, baths, and homework. So she'd beg him to wake her up early so that she could talk with him before he went to work. He'd wake her up, pour them both a cup of hot tea, and they'd sit at the kitchen table and talk. Kim doesn't remember any of the details of those conversations, but she does know that they developed a special relationship in those morning hours. They got to know each other! Isaiah 50:4 says, "He wakens me morning by morning, wakens my ear to listen like one being taught." Are you a morning person? Get up early for some teatime with God! Are you more of a night owl? Then clear some time on your evening schedule to get to know God better. Find a time every day when you can just *be*—when you can be still and be with God.

Remember Who You're Talking With

Begin your time with God by remembering who it is you're talking with. Think about the images of God described in the Bible. Check out John's description of the throne of God in Revelation 4. Or envision God as described in Daniel 7:9, 10:

> As I looked,
> thrones were set in place,

and the Ancient of Days took his seat.

His clothing was as white as snow;

the hair of his head was white like wool.

His throne was flaming with fire,

and its wheels were all ablaze.

A river of fire was flowing,

coming out from before him.

Thousands upon thousands attended him;

ten thousand times ten thousand stood before him.

There's just something about getting on your knees, face to the ground, that helps you get your mind wrapped around the fact that you're coming before the very throne of God in that very instant! When you spend time with God, you're talking with the creator of the universe—God Almighty himself!

Elisabeth Elliot said, "The God who created, names and numbers the stars in the heavens also numbers the hairs of my head . . . He pays attention to the very big things and to the very small ones. What matters to me matters to Him, and that changes my life."[1] If you aren't sure how to start the conversation, check out Psalms for a good model of how you can talk to God. David talked with God the way a man talks to his friend. Some days he felt good, some days he felt discouraged, some days he complained about other people, and some days he even despaired of his life. No matter what he was experiencing, he shared it with God. Like David, pray with raw honesty. And don't be afraid to ask God for what you need. Philippians 4:6 says, "in every thing by prayer and supplication with thanksgiving let your requests be made known unto God." Proverbs 16:3 says, "Commit thy works unto the LORD, and thy thoughts shall be established" (*KJV*). Tell him everything.

Confess Your Sins to God

Ever felt like God seems far away? When we feel that way, the first thing we need to ask ourselves is if there is any unconfessed sin in our lives that may be "blocking" us from hearing him. Sometimes God is silent because he's choosing to be for a reason we don't know. But other times we may not feel connected to God because *we've* allowed sin to choke our relationship with him. So ask yourself, *Is there anything I need to confess?* If something comes to mind, talk to God about it. He knows it all anyway, so you may as well get it all out on the table! Let him love you.

Talk with God Through His Word

Remember: the primary way God talks to us is through his Word. The Bible is the living, breathing Word of God. It speaks to us in amazingly personal ways. As you develop consistent time with God in his Word, there will be times when the Scriptures seem to jump off the page, and you will know in that moment that God is sitting right with you, speaking directly to your situation. We have had countless experiences of asking him a question, sometimes even writing it down in our journals, only to have him answer it minutes later in the most hair-raising, spine-tingling, make-you-jump-up-and-go-*whoa!* kind of way. So open your Bible and talk to him as you go along.

You can start any number of ways. Go to your local Bible bookstore and pick up a study guide on a particular book of the Bible or on a particular topic. A good Bible commentary will give you others' perspectives on the Scriptures you're reading. If you don't understand something, tell God. Say, "Lord, that makes absolutely no sense to me! Help me understand it." If a passage reminds you of something, say, "Lord, that sounds just like what's going on with so-and-so." If a verse convicts you of something you need to confess, say, "God, I'm so sorry. I've done that very thing lately. Forgive me!" If something he commands is particularly difficult for you, say, "Lord, I'm horrible at giving thanks in all circumstances (or rejoicing always, or refraining from gossip, or giving to the poor). Help me improve in this area."

Think about the main theme of what you're reading. Ask yourself, "What is God trying to tell me here? How does this apply to what's going on in my life right now?" Is God giving you any special insight? If so, write it in the margin of your Bible and date it or write it in your journal. Kim's favorite Bible is a hardcover edition of the NIV that she's had since she was about twelve years old. The margins are so full of her own handwriting that it's difficult to find a bare spot to record any new insights on some pages. The binding is starting to fall apart. She knows she should get a new one, but this Bible is a treasure to her. When you study with a Bible like that, you've got a running history of your walk with God. In the same way you may keep love letters or scrapbooks, you can keep a history of your love-relationship with God.

Watch What Happens

After your times with God in prayer and Bible reading, be expectant and watch for what will happen next. It's really tempting to spend a few minutes with God and then walk on through the day without giving God another thought. But Colossians 4:2 says, "Devote yourselves to prayer, being watchful and thankful." Once during a particularly distressful time in Kim's life, she cried out loud to God, "What is my purpose?" Within the next two weeks, she had three calls asking her to be a part of three different areas of ministry to young women!

Know that your prayer has been heard. Know that when you're uttering your prayers, there is a God in Heaven who is listening to you! You may not hear an answer immediately, but your words are heard the very moment you utter them! So be on the lookout for how God will work. Pray . . . watch . . . be thankful.

When You Hear from Him, Obey

In Luke 11:28, Jesus said, "Blessed rather are those who hear the word of God and obey it." Sometimes, when you read a challenging passage of Scripture or when God nudges you through his Holy Spirit, you won't feel like saying yes to God.

Do it anyway.

Kim: I remember one powerful way I learned this lesson. I received an e-mail from a young friend named Megan that I'd met months earlier on a mission trip in Honduras. She was coming back to college in our town in the fall and she needed a place to live. What would I think, she asked, about her living with me?

My gut reaction was "No!" I was very comfortable living alone and having my own space, thank you very much.

But immediately after that thought came the unmistakable nudging of God: "Say yes. This is as much for your own good as it is hers." I knew that I **knew** that it was the voice of God because every selfish bone in my body wanted to say no. I wrote back a "Yes!" before I had time to change my mind. And my obedience paid off. Megan's presence in my home blessed me beyond measure. And on the day Megan pulled out of the driveway at the end of the semester with her car packed with all her belongings, I waved and bawled until her car was out of sight. God taught me a lot through my time with Megan . . . and I would have missed out on it all if I hadn't obeyed what God was leading me to do.

So What's God Saying to You?

We'd all love it if God spoke out loud to us like he did to Samuel (1 Samuel 3). Wouldn't it be great if a great voice from the clouds said, "Sarah, I want you to go to the state college near home next year" or "Kaley, I definitely want you to break up with Jerod." But he doesn't typically do things that way these days (at least he never has with us!). God speaks to us in our minds or in our spirits. When we feel a nudge to call a friend to say we're sorry, or when we're reminded that we should bake some cookies for the elderly man next door, or when we feel convicted about an area of sin in our lives and we're driven to our knees to confess and repent . . . that's often God speaking! Even if we don't hear an actual voice, we can still prepare ourselves to hear from him by being still, by remembering who we're talking with, by confessing our sins, by talking with him through his Word, by watching what happens, and by obeying him when he speaks.

Spending time with God changes us—and it empowers us to change the world for him! Developing an intimate relationship with God will be the most rewarding thing you ever do . . . it is *so* worth your time.

Get Your Shoes On!

Questions for Small Group Reflection

Read these questions and talk about them with your friends—or jot down your own thoughts in your *One Girl Journal*.

1. Do you agree that God still speaks today? If so, how? Does he speak to you? Explain.

2. Hagar called God by the name *El Roi*, which means "the Living One who sees me." How does that make you feel to know that God sees your everyday circumstances?

3. When he left earth, Jesus promised that he would send the Holy Spirit to live inside us and to guide us in the truth. How have you experienced the Holy Spirit in your life?

4. Hebrews 4:12 says, "the word of God is living and active." How have you experienced it "coming to life"—speaking straight to you as you read it? Describe your experience.

5

extreme makeover

> "I don't understand how a woman
> can leave the house without fixing herself
> up a little—if only out of politeness.
> And then, you never know,
> maybe that's the day she has a date with destiny."
> —Coco Chanel[1]

So here's a question for you: How long does it take you to get ready for a date or a special night out with friends? An hour? An hour and a half? *Two?* It sort of depends, doesn't it? Guys may never understand why we can't be ready in the ten minutes it takes them, but what we can't tell them (because, let's face it, we want them to believe we just walk out the door naturally looking this fabulous) is that it takes a *lot* of time to shave, polish, tweeze, exfoliate, moisturize, blush, gloss, and primp! And that doesn't even count the time standing in the closet picking out the right outfit and accessories!

Coco Chanel was right—as a world changer, having your date with destiny takes some preparation. And we're talking an *extreme makeover* here! The good news is, you've already done quite a bit of the planning. You've spent time thinking about your God-given passions. You've written in your journal about the things that make your heart go pitter-patter, what you want your life to be about, and the things you want to be remembered for. You're starting to understand the unique kind of leader you're created to be. You've written your life mission statement. You're developing the practice of listening to God. Now what? How do you actually move forward in accomplishing your goals?

One approach is that you could do nothing. You could sit there and just sort of hope that it all mysteriously unfolds and, *voila!,* all of a sudden you're setting the world on fire!

Bad news: That's generally not the way God works. God is a *planner.* Nothing he does is by accident. The Bible is full of examples in which we read about how God *plans* things so they happen exactly as he wants. The psalmist knew what he was talking about when he wrote, "The plans of the LORD stand firm forever, the purposes of his heart through all generations" (Psalm 33:11). So don't just wait around. Join God in being intentional about the action steps you want to take to change the world. And we've got a suggestion for step one.

Joshua had a clear mission from God: After the death of Moses, God chose Joshua to lead the Israelites into the promised land. He told Joshua to be strong and courageous. He told him never to depart from God's law—to meditate on it day and night. He told Joshua that he'd be with him wherever Joshua went. So Joshua gave the orders to the people: "Get your supplies ready. Three days from now you will cross the Jordan here to go in and take possession of the land the LORD your God is giving you for your own" (Joshua 1:11).

Then the day before they're to cross over to the land they've waited forty years to possess, what does Joshua say to the Israelites? "Pick up all of this trash, people! Let's leave this place the way we found it forty years ago!"?

Nope. How about, "There will be an additional charge for luggage weighing over fifty pounds"?

Not quite. Do you think it was, "Did everyone use the bathroom? It's a long way to the next rest stop!"?

Of course not. But look closely at what he *did* say: "Consecrate yourselves, for tomorrow the LORD will do amazing things among you" (Joshua 3:5).

What?! They've waited forty years for this moment, and he tells them now, at the eleventh hour, to *consecrate* themselves? That sounds like asking a child to clean her room the night before her first trip to Disney World! What does it even mean to consecrate yourself anyway? Well if it was important enough for Joshua to tell the Israelites to do it just before claiming the promised land, we figured it was worth looking up. *Zondervan Handbook to the Bible* explains that *consecrate* means to "prepare yourselves before God, by . . . self-examination in light of what God requires."[2] To consecrate means to set apart, to make holy, to sanctify, and to purify. Those are all good definitions, but we prefer to think of it as the ultimate extreme makeover.

Have you ever had an experience like this? You've got a big night planned (like a date with your boyfriend or a movie with the girls). Your schedule has been jam-packed all day, and now you find yourself with just enough time to get home, change clothes, and spray on some perfume before heading back out the door. You give yourself a quick glance in the mirror and see that the makeup you applied when you left the house that morning is looking a little worse for the wear. What you could really use is some time to wash your face and start all over, but you don't have that luxury. So you brush some powder on the T-zone, reapply some eye makeup, and throw on some lip gloss. You give one last glance in the mirror, shrug your shoulders, say, "good enough," and head out the door.

We've all had moments like that. Sometimes we just don't have a choice! Everyone else may think you look great, but *you* know it's just a patch job. You know that you're struggling to actually see anything from behind that clumpy mess of fresh mascara applied on top of the old. You know that what your skin is really screaming for is a good apricot scrub and a cool cucumber moisturizer.

Any beauty expert worth her weight in retinoids will tell you that the steps of good skin care are:

Step 1: Cleanse

Step 2: Exfoliate

Step 3: Moisturize

Step 4: Apply

Think of consecration as the cleansing, exfoliating, and moisturizing. It's about washing off the dirt, sloughing off the dead parts, and quenching yourself with God's Word. In the same way that a good skin-care routine helps your makeup look better and last longer, being consecrated and purified on the inside supports your world-changing plan. This chapter is about both—it's about first doing some deep pore cleansing and then applying your plan to a fresh surface.

Get the Bugs Out!

One of the best stories we've heard about consecration actually came from one of Claudia's first-grade students. Chris came bursting into class the first day after the Christmas holiday break, announcing, "Hey, Mrs. Mitchell, it's a new year, and it will be my turn for Show and Tell today!" The class groaned. Chris was, let's say, a very *verbal* seven-year-old. He started almost every sentence with, "I gotta tell ya," and a long, drawn out story would follow until the class was in a glaze-eyed stupor.

Indeed, it *was* Chris's turn for Show and Tell that day. Unlike the other students who shared from their place on the floor, Chris stood and walked to the front of the classroom like he was marching to the music of "Pomp and Circumstance." The students rolled their eyes, and Claudia checked the big clock on the classroom wall. They all knew this was going to be a long story. He carefully took a folded piece of paper from his pocket and held it up. It was a picture he had drawn of a house with a big yellow sun in the corner. Claudia said, "How nice, Chris. Is that your house?"

"Yes, Mrs. Mitchell, this is my house. But it didn't always look like this. *I gotta tell ya . . .*"

He went on, "My dad works all day, so when we found out we got to move to this beautiful house, we had to move at night. It was very dark the night we moved, and it was really cold and rainy. When we got to the house, my dad carried my sister, and my mom held my hand because I'm too big to carry. It was dark in the house. My dad said, 'Chris, take your little sister and sit on the couch while I find the light switch.'

"Well, when he turned on the light, there were bugs *everywhere!* I gotta tell ya, there were bugs on the wall, on the floor, and on the couch! My mom screamed, 'EVERYBODY ON THE PORCH!'

"The porch was safe—no bugs. And my dad had a plan. He knew we might run into some problems, so he had a bomb in the car."

At this point Chris had the students' full attention (as well as the teacher's!) and he knew it. He began to pace in front of the room with his hands behind his back. He continued, "My dad told us he was going to set off a bomb in the house to kill the bugs and it would not be safe to sleep inside. He took my mom and sister to sleep in the car, leaving me on the porch all alone. I gotta tell ya, I was scared, I was cold, and . . . I cried. I just plain cried right there on the porch. Then my dad came. He had a big mattress and blankets and pillows. He told me to lay down and he laid down with me. He put his arms around me and held me all night. I gotta tell ya, that's the best night's sleep I ever had! In the morning, the bugs were gone and our house was clean and beautiful."

Chris received the only standing ovation for Show and Tell that Claudia can remember from all her years of teaching. We think of Chris and his dad's bug bomb when we hear the word "consecrate." Consecration simply means a trip to the porch to get the bugs out. When God tells us to consecrate ourselves because tomorrow he's going to do amazing things among us, he's telling us to get rid of the bugs.

We don't know what the "bugs" are in your life—but you do. You know what particular sins, habits, and bad attitudes infest your life and keep you from being a clean dwelling place for God's Spirit. Perhaps you've begun to dabble in some stuff that you always swore you'd never be a part of. Maybe for you it's selfishness or gossip or lying or cheating or envy. Maybe you're hanging on to an old hurt and your inability to forgive has turned your heart bitter. Maybe you've gone farther with that boy than you ever meant to and now you don't know how to turn back. Maybe you've gotten so used to drinking at parties that you're not sure you remember how to have a good time without it. Maybe you're hurting so much on the inside that you find yourself caught in a cycle of self-injury.

Before you can fulfill God's plans for you to change the world, you need to look those bugs straight in the face and get rid of them. Hebrews 12:1 says, "Let us throw off everything that hinders and the sin that so easily entangles, and let us run with perseverance the race marked out for us." Now's the time to fumigate, girlfriend! To be a world changer, to claim the promised land God has for you, you've got to spend some time on the porch. You need time alone with your spiritual Father, confessing your sins. Just like Chris's dad did, God comes alongside us as we exterminate the bugs in our lives. Isaiah 54:10 says, "'Though the mountains be shaken and the hills be removed, yet my unfailing love for you will not be shaken nor my covenant of peace be removed,' says the LORD, who has compassion on you." The Hebrew word for "compassion" is *racham,* which means "to soothe; to cherish; to love deeply." [3] With great compassion, God comes to *you* on the porch—soothing you, cherishing you, loving you deeply—so you can live a new life.

Your Mulligan

Have you ever heard of the golf term *mulligan?* If you make a mistake in golf, taking a mulligan means getting a second chance at another swing—it's a do-over. Jesus died so you could have a mulligan! If you're hanging on to unforgiveness, he died to release you from it. If you've gone too far with that boy, he died so that you can become sexually pure again. If you've become a slave to using alcohol or other drugs, he died to give you back your sobriety. If you're self-injuring, he died to heal your internal scars and to free you from the cycle. You *can* turn to Jesus right now and ask his help to change it all. You can decide right now to never go back to the way things were.

Our friend Courtney did. Courtney seemed to walk through life with a chip on her shoulder. She was a high school student who'd moved to a big city from a small town in the Midwest and had gotten involved with the wrong crowd. She'd become rebellious in a lot of ways, and she looked the part. She'd changed from an apparently innocent, soft-hearted girl to a dark, hardened cynic. But one summer she had a moment with the Lord in which she decided she'd never return to the rebellious ways she'd been living in. This doesn't mean that she didn't make other kinds of mistakes later, but she really did change. Courtney never went back to *that* point at which she'd been. With God's help, she cleaned her life up and then made a plan. Courtney made new friends at school, decided to live in obedient submission to her parents, reconnected with her youth group, and established a daily routine with God. Courtney now leads the junior high dance ministry at a large church in Chicago. Her heart has remained soft, and she has *never* returned to that dark place.

No matter what sins you're dealing with—no matter if they seem really huge to you or really small—Jesus can handle them. Like Courtney did, you can make a decision right now to start over. Jesus died so that you can have a mulligan. If you can get that, it will change who you are for the rest of your life.

Press On

King David knew what it's like to spend time "on the porch," confessing sin and asking God's forgiveness. He experienced God's consecration and described it this way in Psalm 40:1, 2:

> I waited patiently for the LORD;
> he turned to me and heard my cry.
> He lifted me out of the slimy pit,
> out of the mud and mire;
> he set my feet on a rock
> and gave me a firm place to stand.

After you spend time getting the bugs out, you'll still sometimes face feelings of defeat. Resist them! That's exactly where the enemy would like you to be: still wallowing in the slimy pit David talked about. You'll never be effective in changing the world if you're stuck in mud and mire! So when those feelings assault you, remember that God has lifted you out of that pit. Follow the apostle Paul's example, who wrote in Philippians 3:12-14:

I press on to take hold of that for which Christ Jesus took hold of me . . . I do not consider myself yet to have taken hold of it. But one thing I do: Forgetting what is behind and straining toward what is ahead, I press on toward the goal to win the prize for which God has called me heavenward in Christ Jesus.

After you've consecrated yourself, make a conscious choice to forget what is behind and press on toward the goal!

If you ask a world-class runner what she thinks about during the race, we can guess what her answer will be: the finish line. In those final moments before her race begins, she dismisses all the distractions and fixes her eyes on the goal. She doesn't think about all the races she hasn't won. She doesn't check out her competition. She doesn't scan the stands for her parents. Like a racehorse with blinders on, she has a single focus: the finish line.

What's the finish line you are focusing on? Grab your journal for a moment and write down a specific goal. It could be a personal goal, a spiritual goal, or a goal that fits under the umbrella of your life mission. Whatever it is, write it down. Then jot down some notes about the steps it will take to get there.

Not quite sure where to start? Here are a few examples from some world-changing girls we know that will model for you how you can start striving toward your own specific goals.

Jessica, a college student friend of ours, found herself at a frat party, drinking alcohol for the first time in her life. Her defenses were weakened, and she ended up doing things she would never have otherwise done. She felt awful afterward—embarrassed, guilty, and discouraged. After talking together, we spent time on our knees in a prayer of consecration. Jessica left our time together brand new in the eyes of God. She drove a stake into the ground that day, declaring she'd never go back. Sure, she'll make other mistakes in life, but she will never drink alcohol at a frat party again—that was her goal.

But to ensure her success, she needed more than just an idea. She had to devise a plan. This is what she decided:

1. I will meet with a small group of girls for Bible study once a week so they can hold me accountable.

2. Until I turn twenty-one, I will *not* drink alcohol and, under no circumstances, at a party. If I *do* go to parties, I will take a diet soda with me and will not let go of it all night.

3. I will never go to a party without one of my accountability friends.

Pretty good plan, we'd say. How will Jessica change the world? For starters, she's bringing light into the dark places of her campus.

Here's another example from our friend Sylva's life. When Sylva was a senior in high school, she heard about a local grant that would be awarded for a project commemorating the life of Martin Luther King Jr. Noticing that her high school's concrete block walls were painted a drab battleship gray, art-loving Sylva had an idea: she wanted to paint a wall of her school with a mural depicting images from Martin Luther King Jr.'s speeches. But of course she couldn't just go off and start painting the walls of a public, taxpayer-funded institution! What she needed was a solid plan in order to write a good grant proposal. So starting with the finish line in mind (a vision of a mural that would not only honor Martin Luther King Jr. but would also beautify the school), she created a plan:

1. Find an appropriate wall for the mural. (She chose one in the hallway near the indoor swimming pool.)

2. Sketch out on paper an idea of what the mural would look like (images from Martin Luther King Jr.'s various speeches).

3. Meet with the principal to share the vision and get approval. (He loved the idea!)

4. Research the cost of paint and supplies (including free pizza for the students during paint day!).

5. Write the grant proposal, including her vision, specifics about the funding required ($600), and the benefit to the community.

6. Recruit a team (painters, people to photograph the day, someone from the school paper to write a story, and a cleanup team) using flyers, morning announcements, and so on.

Now that's a solid example of a plan!

Your plan will look different from Jessica's and Sylva's based on the goal you've got in mind. But whatever the goal, remember these three important criteria. A good plan should:

1. Start with the end in mind.

2. Be specific.

3. Include deadlines.

So keep your eye on the goal. Think about how long each step will take, and assign specific dates by which you need to achieve each step in order to go to the next one. We'll talk more about how you can work with others in chapter 7, but you can start thinking about that a bit now too. For example, does one of your action steps involve making phone calls, but *you* get nervous picking up the phone and asking for help? Enlist the help of a friend who's a Lollipop Twirler! Does another step include managing finances? That's where you need to call on a friend who's a Lollipop Saver. Don't try to take on too much by yourself . . . get your friends on board too!

Dream Big

Frances Havergal had a goal in mind during a five-day visit at a friend's home. Ten others were staying there too—five of them were not believers in Jesus, and the other five were believers but (as Frances described them in her journal) were "not rejoicing Christians." She prayed, "Lord, give me all in this house!"

She wrote in her journal that every single one received a blessing before her visit ended—and that two of them put their faith in Jesus at nearly midnight on the last night of Frances's visit! After the women left her room, Frances felt so much joy and gratitude to God for his answer to her prayers that she couldn't sleep. She felt inspired to follow God all the more boldly in her life. That night in 1874 was when she penned the words of the now-famous hymn "Take My Life and Let it Be." [4] Read these words about consecration, and make her prayer your own:

Take my life, and let it be consecrated, Lord, to Thee.
Take my moments and my days; let them flow in ceaseless praise.
Take my hands, and let them move at the impulse of Thy love.
Take my feet, and let them be swift and beautiful for Thee.

Take my voice, and let me sing always, only, for my King.
Take my lips, and let them be filled with messages from Thee.
Take my silver and my gold; not a mite would I withhold.
Take my intellect, and use every power as Thou shalt choose.

Take my will, and make it Thine; it shall be no longer mine.

Take my heart, it is Thine own; it shall be Thy royal throne.

Take my love, my Lord, I pour at Thy feet its treasure store.

Take myself, and I will be ever, only, all for Thee. [5]

Get Your Shoes On!

Questions for Small Group Reflection

Read these questions and talk about them with your friends—or jot down your own thoughts in your *One Girl Journal*.

1. Describe in your own words what *consecrate* means.

2. What "bugs" do you feel like you need to clean out of your life? If you feel comfortable, share with the group.

3. How do you feel after confessing your sins to God? Do you believe that you are forgiven?

4. What's one goal you want to aim for? What steps need to take place for that goal to become a reality? How can others help you accomplish those steps?

6

passing the punch-bowl test

There's a great scene in the hit movie *My Big Fat Greek Wedding* in which Toula has an eye-opening conversation with her mom. Toula is upset because her father has denied her dream of going to college. He's unwavering in his opinion that his daughter should simply work in the family restaurant until she settles down and marries a nice Greek man. In the scene, Toula sits on her bed crying while her mother, Maria, tries to comfort her. Maria tells Toula not to worry, saying that she'll talk to her father. Toula still feels hopeless—her father believes that the man is the head of the house and that his decision is always *final*. Maria, taking Toula's chin in her hand and pulling her close, looks her in the eyes and tells her not to worry: "The man is the head," Maria says, "but the woman is the neck. And she can turn the head *any way she wants.*" [2]

Being a leader means having *influence*. The question is: What kind of influence are you going to have?

Character Matters

A bit like Maria acting as the influential "neck" in her family, professor Holly Brower believes that, "The essence of leadership is influencing people to go in some direction. You are always leading," she told us. "There are always people watching you." [3] Holly knows a thing or two about leadership. She's an associate professor at Wake Forest University and teaches classes on the subject; she's also worked in youth ministry and has been involved with nonprofit organizations since childhood. Holly believes that having good *character* is nonnegotiable when it comes to leadership.

So what is good character? Surely it doesn't mean being perfect—we all have flaws and shortcomings. Character has often been defined as, "Who you are when no one is looking." There's just one big problem with that definition: there's *never* a time when no one is looking! God always sees you. He sees your outward actions and your inner thoughts and feelings . . . even in those secret moments when no one else is around. Character has to do both with our public life and those private moments, when it's just us and God.

Character may be tough to define precisely, but we all know, deep in our heart of hearts, when we're exhibiting good character and when we're not. Writer and pastor Andy Stanley defines it this way: "Character is the will to do what's right even when it's hard." He says, "Your gifts and determination may dictate your potential, but it is your character that will determine your legacy. You can create an enviable lifestyle by leveraging your leadership skills alone. But you cannot create an enviable life without giving serious attention to who you are on the inside."[4]

Character is about the choices you make that build your reputation, and Holly Brower teaches that you need to establish your reputation from an early age. She suggests imagining your life ten or twenty years into the future and asking yourself, "What do I want people to say about me when I come back to my high school reunion?" Imagine all your friends, acquaintances, and classmates standing around the punch bowl, swapping stories, and saying, "I remember when you . . . " Will they be talking about the party where you got drunk and passed out in the hot tub? About a time you started a nasty rumor about someone? About when you helped them cheat on the chemistry final? Or will they be talking about the time you really inspired them by taking a stand against drinking or the time you defended a social outcast or about the time you refused to cheat (even though they begged you to!)?

What stories do you want people to tell about you around that punch bowl? How do you want to be remembered? If you aren't sure what to zero in on when it comes to developing your own character, Galatians 5:22, 23 is a good place to start. This list of the fruit of the Spirit highlights key character traits that we would all be wise to strive for: love, joy, peace, patience, kindness, goodness, faithfulness, gentleness, and self-control. This list can make an excellent punch-bowl test, if you ask us! Knowing what you want people to say about you twenty years from now will bring focus and clarity to the choices you make today, tomorrow, and the next day.

Tools to Keep Your *Twords* in Check

"Character is personal, but it is not private," Andy Stanley says. "Everybody who knows you has an opinion about the kind of person you are. You might as well let them know the kind of person you are striving to become."[5] Who can *you* share your character goals with? Think about a woman you respect and who lives out the character that you want to follow—a parent, teacher, friend, or mentor. She doesn't need to be somebody with your same interests or life vision, but she does need to be somebody with spiritual maturity who will bring a biblical perspective to your relationship. Once you've decided on who that woman is, sit down together and have an honest conversation. Tell her, "These are the specific character traits I'm working on, and I'd like your help in developing them."

Ask your friend to do something that's really tough—call you out when she spots you breaking one of your own convictions. It won't be fun—it will probably feel pretty embarrassing. It might even make you mad. But when your friend holds you accountable, remember that she's helping you become the person you want to be. She's helping to shape the stories that will be told about you around the punch bowl at that high school reunion!

Along with having a friend by your side, cheering you on as you strive to live with punch-bowl worthy character, you can also do some things on your own to keep your integrity in check. Recently we saw a pastor on TV who challenged his congregation to stop complaining. He asked everyone in his church to join him in wearing a rubber bracelet; whenever anyone caught themselves complaining, they were to give the bracelet a hard snap. Ouch! That temporary sting of the bracelet was meant to remind participants to strive hard to quit the complaining habit. If anybody went twenty consecutive days without complaining, they could switch their bracelet to the other wrist.

Claudia: I love that bracelet idea because it shows a serious commitment to break a bad habit. But to be sure, there are other less painful ways to develop your character too! Playing golf is an excellent character builder, and I decided to learn to play golf so that I could communicate better with the men in my life. Golf has its own language, and my husband and sons speak it fluently! Their vocabulary is peppered with words like **bogey, birdie, eagle, par,** and **mulligan.** So I've been learning the language and also a bit about golf etiquette (such as "Don't talk when someone is putting," "Wearing tank tops on the course is **not** OK," and "Don't drive the cart on the green!"). I've learned the hard way that you should always hang onto the cart when the driver is going around a curve, you should never put a candy bar in the pocket of your golf bag on a sunny day, and you should always look to see where you last put the golf clubs before driving your car into the garage.

One day, a golfer friend introduced me to a concept that has stayed with me. After hitting a ball into some trees, he said, "Oops. My **twords** was off." Noting my quizzical look, he translated the term **twords** for me as slang for **towards**—as in, "My aim was a little off of what I was aiming towards."

Do you ever feel like your **twords** is a little off? Like your life is just not going in the direction that you planned or you're just not quite the person you want to be? Have you ever asked yourself, "How did I end up **here?**" Do you ever feel like you're just not quite hitting the mark? I feel that way sometimes—we all do. That's because there's this big ravine: a gap between who we are today and who we want to become. Sometimes it seems deep and long and impassable. It's like golf. No matter how much I want to be the next Tigress Woods, just showing up with the right golf equipment won't do it. Having the right heart and all the "want to" in the world won't do it. There is no magic bullet—nothing you can do that'll instantly move yourself from where you are today to who you want to become. So how do we cross that *ravine? How do we keep our **twords**?*

*You cannot stay on this side of the ravine and get to who you want to be. You need a bridge—a discipline bridge. And you must choose to walk across it. You must choose the path of discipline. The difference between me and Tiger Woods is that I want to hit the golf ball—but not badly enough to do what he does . . . which is to hit 600 balls a day! True discipline is wanting it badly enough to actually **do** it—and to do it even when it's hard.*

Whether it's getting a mentor to hold you accountable, snapping your wrist with a bracelet, or some other creative idea, find a tool to help you shape the person you are into the person you want to be—with God's help, of course! Character does matter. The old saying is true: actions speak louder than words. Leadership is about more than influencing people with your persuasive skills or your charming charisma. It's about the life you live and the example you set. So get some help to keep your *twords* right where you want it to be.

It's Not About You

Of all the important traits that make up good character, the very best and most important of them is servant leadership. No matter what your Lollipop Leadership style is, you are called to follow Jesus' example of servant leadership, and it can boiled down to three simple words: putting others first. Jesus said in Matthew 20:26, 28: "Whoever wants to become great among you must be your servant . . . just as the Son of Man did not come to be served, but to serve."

The most famous example of servant leadership is found in John 13, when Jesus washes his disciples' feet. Can you imagine what that was like for the disciples? We're talking about God incarnate here! God, who set aside all the glory of Heaven and came to this earth to identify with us in our humanity! And here he was, kneeling in front of his friends and washing their dirty, smelly feet. In Jesus' day, walking in sandals on dusty roads meant that feet were very dirty, so foot washing was a job regularly performed by servants. In this scene we see Jesus lowering himself to servant level, performing one of the dirtiest and most humbling jobs possible.

And as if that wasn't enough, listen to the *words* Jesus said to his disciples when he finished washing their feet: "Now that I, your Lord and Teacher, have washed your feet, you also should wash one another's feet. I have set you an example that you should do as I have done for you" (John 13:14, 15). Though we don't literally wash each other's feet today, Jesus' call to his disciples is the same for us: he calls us to serve one another and often to do that in radical ways.

Today we don't ordinarily walk in sandals on dirt roads covered with camel doo-doo and who knows what else. But there are lots of other ways we can serve in amazing humility. For example, we've got a friend who goes directly from school to a nursing home she volunteers at where she paints the fingernails and toenails of the residents. She is a modern-day foot washer. So is another teen girl we know who volunteers at the hospital, delivering flowers and emptying bedpans. So is seventeen-year-old Jessica, who—while on a mission trip in Haiti—learned about servant leadership by holding and rocking babies in an orphanage and by hand-washing endless piles of dirty laundry. [6]

So is fourteen-year-old Kayla, who served five- and six-year-olds in the inner city simply by holding them, playing with them, and loving on them. She says, "If you were to ask me what I learned in the inner city, I'd have to say that those kids taught me more than I could ever teach them . . . I may not have learned much theological stuff, but I can say one thing: I learned more about Jesus in that one week than ever before.

Why? I saw him. He was in every child. In each face I saw my Lord . . . I learned how to love like Jesus. I learned to look in a face that I would previously think belonged to just a little kid with a dirty face and feel like I was about to cry from the tug on my heart. That tug was love."

Kayla says, "The kids taught me that it's not what we say, it's how we act that makes a difference in people's lives. Sure it's great to tell people about God. But why not show him through your actions too? The best way to do that is to love them. Love the unlovables. Carry the untouchables. Let little children sleep on your shoulder and brush their fingers through your hair."[7]

That's modern-day feet washing. When you're willing to set aside your own interests and spend time putting others first and when they can see how much you care for them, then they'll be motivated to follow you . . . and to follow Jesus.

You may not have heard of Agnes Bojaxhiu, but she was a true servant leader. By the time she was twelve years old, she was captivated by stories of missionaries, and at age eighteen she made the life-changing decision to become one. Surely Agnes must have been concerned about the same things on the mind of any teen girl. Perhaps she thought about boys ("How do I get him to notice me?" . . . "Is this guy the one I could end up marrying?"). At eighteen, she might have been concerned about the monumental life changes that the next five to ten years could bring ("Where will I live?" . . . "Will I concentrate on my career first, and wait to have a family later?" . . . "Where will I settle down?"). But she answered God's call and left her home country, never to see her own mother again. She sacrificed marriage and having her own family and the possibility of a more prestigious life for the sake of devoting herself to those she was sent to serve. She lived among the poor, choosing to serve the hungry, homeless, lonely, and sick in the slums.

You may know Agnes better by the name she took in her mission work:

Mother Teresa. Though she became world famous in the later years of her life, don't ever forget that Mother Teresa was once a teen girl—*just like you*. And for decades she served God without fame, without notice, without a recognizable name. She was a true servant leader who has inspired people around the globe to truly live out Jesus' call to put others first.

World Changers Are . . .

In addition to having good character and servant-leader attitudes, the best world changers have some other traits in common. World changers are:

Courageous

Kim: Late one night my friend Robin and I were sitting in her car in an empty parking lot, drinking five-dollar caramel macchiatos and discussing how we "talk a good talk" about following God, but we felt like we do very little in practice. We wondered, "Are we really being the hands and feet of Jesus? Are we doing enough?"

At that moment we noticed a man riding through the parking lot on a bicycle. He stopped to pick through a restaurant to-go box that had been left on the pavement. We watched as he picked up another container and started eating someone's discarded leftovers. Robin said, "Oh, Kim, he's eating it. What are we going to do? What are we going to do? I don't have any more money on me."

"I have some cash," I said, "but I don't know . . . I mean, I don't want to hurt his pride or offend him. Besides, maybe he's dangerous."

But Robin's the kind of person who just takes risks. Before I knew it, Robin grabbed the cash from my hand and drove toward the man on the bicycle. We pulled up beside him and Robin handed him the folded money. Very gently she said, "I don't want to offend you, but I thought you could use this."

With tears in his eyes, the man answered, "Oh, I'm not poor . . . I'm not rich, but I'm not poor." (He clearly was much poorer than we were!)

As we drove away, Robin said to me, "Kim, we think we were put here tonight for **him**. *But really he was put here for* **us**.*" God gave us an opportunity to serve. And Robin's a great example in my life of someone who leads the way in taking every opportunity to serve that she can find. Without Robin's courage I wouldn't have experienced the joy of what God had in store for us in that parking lot.*

To be an effective leader, you don't have to be the most intelligent girl in the world. You don't need to have the most outgoing personality. You don't need to be the prettiest, funniest, or most creative. But you do need courage. You need to be willing to step out of your comfort zone and *do* whatever that big, bold, risky job is that God has set in front of you. Make the phone call. Introduce yourself to that person you'd like to meet. Volunteer a few hours of your time somewhere. Offer to lead the next Bible study.

So what about you? Do you have the courage to just *do* what's before you? To take a big leap? To be that person who steps out in faith? Professor Holly Brower urges young women to "Just do *something*. There's plenty to do—you can volunteer at a hospital or a nursing home or read to kids in an after-school program . . . It's about stepping out into the risky unknown, leading, taking initiative, making a difference in people's lives. It doesn't have to be this great, earth-shattering thing to start, or you'll end up at age sixty-five going, 'I really wanted to do something!'"

Humble

Kim: One year I decided, despite having no musical ability at all, to learn to play the fiddle. I got an instrument, but it needed restringing. I, of course, had no idea how to do that! So I went into a store that sold and repaired violins and asked the older man in the shop if he could show me how to restring my pawn-shop fiddle. He chuckled a bit, but he restrung A, then told me in a thick accent, "G looks veery zuzpeezious, alzo." So he restrung G and then taught me how to do it myself in the future.

As I was leaving the shop, he said, "You should get a new case zoon, because theez one eez in veery bad shape." I explained that the case was borrowed. Then he held up one finger and said, "Vait a minute . . . I have a case for you." He walked to the back of the shop and returned with a case for me. Then he said the chin rest on my instrument was also loose, and gave me a pin to tighten it with.

His kindness really touched me. I was curious about his story, so later on I did what any curious person would do—I looked him up online. I immediately figured out why he chuckled when I asked if he could restring the fiddle! It turns out that he was a famous violinist from Moscow who has been a symphony conductor and now makes violins for international clients and famous violinists!

I was struck by his humility. That man had treated **me** as if I were his most important customer—not even once did he hint at his accomplishments.

Humble leaders are people who don't like to talk about themselves. They love to talk about the project they're involved in, and they love to give credit to the people on their team. They're gracious, modest, and real team players. How about you? Are you a humble leader? Do you need to be in the limelight, or are you quick to recognize your teammates when things go well? Harry Truman once said, "It is amazing what you can accomplish if you do not care who gets the credit."[8] To be a world changer, practice the art of humility.

Willing to Be Led

Good leaders know they don't have all the answers. They know themselves well—both their strengths *and* their weaknesses. They have open minds to others' opinions. They're curious and always looking to improve themselves. Proverbs 15:32 says, "He who ignores discipline despises himself, but whoever heeds correction gains understanding." Which part of this proverb best describes you? How do *you* react when a friend offers a different way of doing things or tries to lovingly correct you? We have to admit, we don't always handle this well. We need to fight the need to be right, to do it our way. We don't take criticism well. But we're learning!

Kim: One time a good friend of mine told me that she was worried about me—she said I'd seemed angry a lot of the time lately. I immediately snapped back, "I am NOT angry!"

She dropped it, and we walked away from the situation still friends but with a big, unresolved issue between us.

After cooling down and taking some time to reflect on what my friend said, I started to wonder about what impressions I'd been making on people lately. I knew my friend loved me and, like Mary Poppins said, "a spoonful of sugar helps the medicine go down." I realized that my friend was **right**. (Gulp. Can you hear the sound of a spoonful of pride being swallowed?) I needed to be willing to really listen.

So what about you? Are you able to take second chair while someone else takes the lead? Are you able to put aside your need to be in charge and work as a true team player? When a friend has the courage to point out a flaw, realize that they want the best for you! Take the time to examine the truth they've shared, and remember you aren't perfect. If you want to lead, you've got to be willing to be led.

Visionary

Imagine your parents telling you that you've impressed them so much with your academic work this year that they've decided to take you on a fabulous trip. You're leaving tomorrow, they say, and you need to pack tonight. But there's one hitch: they won't tell you where you're going. It's a surprise, and they won't even give you a hint. How will you pack? If it's the Caribbean, a bathing suit and a toothbrush might be all you need. If, on the other hand, it's a trip to Aspen, you'll need your parka, ski pants, gloves, earmuffs, and snow boots. If it's an African safari, you'll need your hiking boots and binoculars. If it's Paris, you'll need your French-English dictionary, skinny jeans, and stilettos. With no idea of the destination, you've got only one option—pack everything!

That's what it's like to work under a leader with no vision. If you're a leader without a clear picture of the desired outcome, you end up trying to pack it all in. You try to think of all the things you might possibly need to do in order to reach some unknown destination, and you end up burning out. The luggage is too heavy to carry. Little by little, teammates start disembarking at each station. They pack it in and head for home. They lose steam for the project because they had no sense of where you're all headed.

Take this scenario, for example. Let's say you and some friends attend a youth conference. During the course of the weekend, you get all fired up about missions. You hear a missionary from a third-world country speak about children being kidnapped and trained in guerilla warfare. You see pictures of elementary-age kids with guns in their hands. Your heart is so stirred for these kids that you and your friends decide to go back home and make a difference: you want to raise money to support the rescue of these children. You decide that as soon as you get back home, you'll call the local supermarket and see if you can rent a hot dog stand for a weekend to raise some money. One person will make posters, another will call the supermarket, and another friend will purchase the supplies. You all divvy up the rest of the jobs. You're psyched . . . ready to really help those kids.

But then what happens? Everyone gets back home and settles in to their routines of school, work, and extracurricular activities. Somehow everyone forgets about the pictures of those children sleeping in the streets. Nobody really carries the banner. You and your friends lose the vision.

So how did that great idea die? It wasn't because you or your friends didn't care enough! But it was probably because one of you needed to step up to the plate, grab that vision, and carry it high. One of you needed to have that destination firmly in your sights, helping the others to keep their eyes on it too.

Can you be that person? Are others drawn to help you on your mission because you're able to stir their hearts, to get them to dream big, to paint a picture of the end goal? You *can* be a leader that inspires a vision in the hearts of your teammates. And, when the going gets tough, they won't abandon you.

It Takes Guts

Kim: *Remember that story I told you about earlier? Well after we drove away from the hungry man in the empty parking lot that night, I marveled at my friend Robin's courage. I had some extra cash, but I wouldn't have been bold enough to step out. It felt a bit like Moses and Aaron in Exodus, where Aaron had the gift of speaking and Moses had the bag of tricks up his sleeve. I told my friend Robin, "Yeah. I had the green . . . and you had the guts!"*

As we talked about in chapter 3, we all have different leadership styles. God has gifted each of us with different spiritual gifts in order to accomplish his purposes. But no matter what your specific leadership style is, these same things always hold true: to be an effective leader, you must develop good character, an attitude of servant leadership, courage, and humility. You must be willing to be led, and you must inspire a vision. And you need to care about you character, even when no one but God is looking. Being a world-changing leader takes more than just a dream— it takes guts.

"A good leader motivates,
doesn't mislead, doesn't exploit.
GOD cares about honesty in the workplace;
your business is his business.
Good leaders abhor wrongdoing of all kinds;
sound leadership has a moral foundation.
Good leaders cultivate honest speech;
they love advisors who tell them the truth.
An intemperate leader wreaks havoc in lives;
you're smart to stay clear of someone like that.
Good-tempered leaders invigorate lives;
they're like spring rain and sunshine"
(Proverbs 16:10-15, *The Message*).

Get Your Shoes On!

Questions for Small Group Reflection

Read these questions and talk about them with your friends—or jot down your own thoughts in your *One Girl Journal*.

1. How important do you think it is for a leader to have good character? Have you ever discovered a major character flaw in someone who was leading you? Without naming names, describe the situation. How did that's person's poor character change your feelings about following under his or her leadership?

2. Andy Stanley defines character as "the will to do what's right even when it's hard." Describe a time when you had to do the right thing, even though it was hard.

3. How would you define good character? Imagine you were talking with someone who had no idea what this term meant— how would you explain it?

4. Think about "the punch-bowl test." What are three character traits you'd most want to be remembered for at a future high school reunion?

5. What can servant leadership look like today? Brainstorm ideas together or share something you've done recently to lead by serving.

7

burpees are better together

> "What I can do, you cannot. What you can do, I cannot. But together we can do something beautiful for God."
> —Mother Teresa [1]

A little while ago, one of us (we've tried to block out how it all started) got this crazy idea that we should start working out. Our church was starting a fitness ministry, and our friend was recruiting test subjects (a.k.a. guinea pigs) before rolling it out to the masses. The gentleman who designs the workout routines is a former Navy SEAL and scours fitness Web sites to come up with the latest methods of torture *(ahem,* we mean, *physical training).*

The first couple of days Cheryl (our coach) took it pretty easy on us, but by the third day she told us we were going to do *burpees. Sounds cute,* we thought. *Maybe it entails making deep guttural noises in order to tone our necks.* Then she demonstrated one for us. Turns out it has nothing to do with the throat. It's kind of like a squat thrust (if you know what those are), except even harder! If you've ever done one, you know it goes something like this:

1. Do a push-up (*boy* style!).
2. Keeping your hands in push-up position, quickly move your legs to a squat.
3. Jump in the air with arms above head.
4. Drop back to a squat.
5. Extend your legs back to push-up position and do a push-up again.
6. Repeat rapidly until you lose the will to live.

Burpees are a killer! We learned that they're designed to increase strength and *explosiveness.* So what, may we ask, is "explosiveness"? We did a quick thesaurus search, and here are some synonyms: volatility, a likeliness to explode, instability, dangerous, likely to lead to violence or hostility! Yep. That pretty much sums up a burpee.

While doing them we thought we'd never see the end and that, if we did, we'd never again breathe normally. For the next few days after, our entire bodies ached, from our biceps to our calf muscles. But we keep going back for more. Why? Two reasons. First, because we know it's good for us (which in itself, let's be honest, would not be a good enough reason). Second, we've discovered that *burpees are better together.* Through the pain and panting, we've developed a special camaraderie. Sometimes the only thing that gets us out of bed and to the gym by 6:30 AM to endure it all over again is simply the knowledge that our burpee buddy will be there right alongside us, encouraging and supporting us all the way.

The Girlfriend Connection

Let's face it: girls are connectors. We need relationships! To paraphrase the words of the sixteenth-century poet John Donne, no girl is an island. Whether it's celebrating our successes or processing our problems, we just have this built-in need to talk it through with someone—to share life with others.

Claudia: One of my favorite memories of girlfriends connecting in a powerful way was when I taught a kindergarten Sunday school class at my church, and it just happened to be made up entirely of girls. I started the class by asking the girls if they had any prayer requests, expecting the usual sick pet or ailing grandma response. Lydia, a tiny little thing with huge eyes brimming with tears, got out of her seat to stand beside me and held my hand. "I need you to pray. My best doll in the whole world has been taken away, and I need you to pray I get her back."

Any girl can relate to this kind of pain. Sure you're all grown up now and you may have a hard time identifying with the pain of losing a favorite doll. But what about other, more "big-girl" losses? Have you ever lost a relationship with a parent or a sibling because of a breakup in your family? Have you ever lost your athletic dreams due to an injury? Have you ever lost your innocence to a boy who once swore he'd love you for always and a day and now won't give you the time of day? Have you ever lost a friend with whom you once shared everything including lip gloss, shoes, and your deepest secrets? Have you ever lost your good reputation in a single, foolish decision? Have you ever lost a loved one to cancer?

Claudia: One loss in particular brings tears to my eyes whenever I remember it. I was in high school and was dating the senior class president and star quarterback. He was going to take me to the prom, but we got into a fight just before, and he ended up asking my best friend instead. It was the worst thing that had ever happened to me up until then. Maybe you know this kind of pain. Have you ever had a crush on a guy, only to find out that he doesn't give you a second thought? Or have you ever had a boyfriend break up with you, only to have people tell you, "Just get over it," "There are more fish in the sea," "Move on!" or "Forget about him—these are the best years of your life!"? (I remember thinking at the time that if these were the best years of my life, I'd hate to see what was coming!).

On the night of the prom, I found myself home alone, staring out my window, and feeling very sorry for myself. I imagined my ex-best friend and ex-boyfriend all dressed up, standing under the photographer's gazebo arm-in-arm, dancing closely, kissing . . .

Just when all that self-torture was about to get the best of me, two acquaintances (not friends, really—just a couple of girls I barely knew from youth group) showed up at my doorstep. They'd heard that I, too, didn't have a prom date, and they invited me to cruise around town with them and to go back to one of their places for a slumber party. I said yes, and we ended up having an absolute blast! And in between all the fun that night, they also put their arms around me, listened to me, and cried with me. We ended up staying close friends throughout the rest of high school.

Sometimes blessings come out of pain, and one of those blessings is that it allows us to connect with others. We need girlfriend connections. Just like with burpees, we connect with each other in our pain. That's why the story of Lydia losing her doll is universal—whether you're six, sixteen, or sixty, you've lost something that's dear to you at one time or another.

Claudia: I quietly asked young Lydia, "Who took your doll?" As tears slid down her cheeks, she confessed that she had a problem with sucking her thumb. Her mother had taken away her doll until she could give up this habit. She asked her classmates to pray that she could stop sucking her thumb. Claudia looked around at the other five girls who were leaning forward in their seats, nearly breathless in identifying with the pain of a sister. Another girl, Amber, was moved to action. She got out of her seat and put her little hand on Lydia's shoulder. The rest of the girls quickly followed her example. I had such a lump in my throat that I wondered how on earth I was going to be able to lead the girls in prayer. But I didn't have to wonder. Instead I watched as five little girls, eyes closed tightly, held each other while Amber prayed for her friend: "God, please help Lydia stop sucking her thumb. It is really hard, and she needs her doll back. Amen." The power of "girlfriend connection"—the need to align with others to achieve our goals—played out before my eyes.

World Changers Need Teams

It's *God's* Idea

We need teams—people who surround us and support us and work alongside us—because that's how God made us. It's time to face the facts: there are things you're good at . . . and some things you're just *not*. The good news is that God already knows this about you. God made you with specific gifts and talents, and he gave others different gifts and talents. In order to change the world, you'll need the help of others who can step in with their strengths in your areas of weakness.

The girls' camp we coordinate is a place where we need everyone to do what they are gifted to do in order to make the week a success. At camp a big part of the experience is the worship time. This is bad news for Kim because worship, as you may know, includes a lot of singing. Kim loves to sing, but she stinks at it. Seriously—we're talking nails-on-chalkboard quality sound! So Kim would never attempt to lead the girls in worship at camp. But it's a vital part of the camp experience! So what's a good leader to do?

Well, as God would have it, our dear friend Cynthia *loves* to sing— and she's good at it. She loves to put motions to the words so that the girls can more easily remember the songs. She has an energy on stage that lights up the crowd. It's her groove. With Cynthia leading worship, and the rest of us doing what we each do best, camp is more well-rounded and the girls have a much better experience because of it. It's called the body of Christ (check out Romans 12:4-8)—it's how God gifts each person in the church with specific abilities and spiritual gifts so that we can work *together* to get things done. You might even call it a match made in Heaven.

Teams Work

You'll be *much* more effective in living out your mission if you've got a team behind you. You'll be able to do more, faster and better. On the other hand, if you try to do it all on your own, you'll get burned out, discouraged, and the end results will suffer. The early church realized this in Acts 6:1-4, 7:

> In those days when the number of disciples was increasing, the Grecian Jews among them complained against the

Hebraic Jews because their widows were being overlooked in the daily distribution of food. So the Twelve gathered all the disciples together and said, "It would not be right for us to neglect the ministry of the word of God in order to wait on tables. Brothers, choose seven men from among you who are known to be full of the Spirit and wisdom. We will turn this responsibility over to them and will give our attention to prayer and the ministry of the word" . . . So the word of God spread. The number of disciples in Jerusalem increased rapidly, and a large number of priests became obedient to the faith.

As the early church grew, it would have been easy for the key leaders—the apostles—to get caught up in trying to do it all: preaching, teaching, coordinating meetings, serving food to the needy, and so on. But serving food wasn't their skill set or their calling! They realized that their time was better spent by focusing on prayer and teaching the Word. In fact, to not focus on their "one thing" would have been wrong. (Verse 4 says, "It would not be right for us to neglect the ministry of the word of God.") So the early church leaders invited others onboard to focus specifically on helping feed the needy in their church. The result? The Word of God spread, and the number of disciples increased rapidly. Do you think things would've turned out this way if the apostles had tried to do everything themselves? They were only human—they probably would've gotten just as burned out as we would today if we tried to change the world all by ourselves!

It's More Fun!

You'll simply have more fun in this changing-the-world business if you've got a team standing with you. They'll encourage you. They'll support you when the going gets rough. You'll have someone to party with when it's time to celebrate your successes!

In the movie *Lemony Snicket's A Series of Unfortunate Events*, young Violet Baudelaire reads this letter from her parents after she and her siblings have mysteriously been abandoned:

> Dearest Children,
>
> Since we have been abroad we have missed you all so much. Certain events have compelled us to extend our travels . . . At times the world can seem an unfriendly and sinister place, but believe us when we say there is much more good in it than bad . . . And what might seem to be a series of unfortunate events may, in fact, be the first steps of a journey. We hope to have you back in our arms soon, darlings, but in case this letter arrives before our return, know that we love you. It fills us with pride to know that no matter what happens in this life, that you three will take care of each other, with kindness and bravery and selflessness, as you always have. And remember one thing, my darlings, and never forget it: that no matter where we are, know that as long as you have each other, you have your family. And you are home. [2]

Yes, at times the world *can* seem an unfriendly and sinister place (why else would it need changing?). That's why God made us to work in teams. You'll need their support when you have to face any unfortunate events of your own, and they will grow you in ways you've never imagined.

Drafting Your Team

As with sports, building a team starts with choosing your draft picks. When we talk about teams, we're not only talking about the people who will take an active role in helping you with specific projects. We're also talking about the big picture here—the people you choose to surround yourself with on a daily basis who will help you grow into the world-changing woman you want to become. The Bible is chock-full of wisdom about your companions! Proverbs tells us, "As iron sharpens iron, so one man sharpens another" (27:17) and "He who walks with the wise grows wise, but a companion of fools suffers harm" (13:20). And 1 Corinthians 15:33 warns that, "Bad company corrupts good character." So whether you're thinking about the team of people who will help you with world-changing projects or about the family and friends who help shape the inner you, you need to choose your draft picks wisely.

What should you look for in teammates? For starters, look for people who have the same character traits you're trying to develop—people who will pass the punch-bowl test! Beyond that, consider the number one quality employers say they look for when selecting a job candidate: *enthusiasm.* Surround yourself with positive, energetic, can-do attitude people. Who do you think got more done: Tigger or Eeyore? No one likes to be around an Eeyore! And you'll have a hard time changing the world if you're constantly drained by a friend or teammate who brings nothing but negative energy to the table. You need people who catch your vision and believe it can be done.

You also need people who will challenge you (even if you find their objections or different approaches somewhat irritating!). People who love you so much that they're willing to risk offending you in order to see you grow. Danielle is this kind of companion to the prince in the movie *Ever After.* Do you remember the scene where the prince, knowing Danielle's love of literature, takes her to show off his library? When she sees it, she tells him straight up how sad it makes her that he's surrounded by books and does not take advantage of the gift he's been given! She says, "You were born to privilege, and with that comes certain obligations." Struck by her words, he replies, "In all my years of study, not one tutor ever demonstrated the passion you have shown me in the last two days. You have more conviction in one memory than I have in my entire being."[3] Look for teammates like that—people who've got conviction and passion and who aren't afraid to lovingly confront you if needed in order to help you succeed.

Kim: I have a group of young women I frequently get together with for coffee or an occasional slumber party. These women are all world changers—one is a missionary, another is a teacher, another is going on to law school in order to defend defenseless children, another will change the world through her athletic ability, and yet another will do so with her art and photography. These girls have been friends for years. They've developed that special kind of trusting, forever friendship that is built from years of doing life together, from losing the first baby tooth to losing the first boyfriend.

I love our late-night conversations—drinking hot cocoa and licking the batter out of the bowl while the brownies are baking. One of the things that makes my heart swell is watching how lovingly honest these friends are with each other. They all love the Lord and want to make him proud, but they have very different personalities, and they struggle with different challenges. Because of their long-lasting friendship, they're not afraid to be very direct and challenging with each other. Recently one of the girls admitted to dabbling in some questionable territory. A vigorous conversation ensued, with about half of the girls defending one position and the other half the other. Someone said, "You've believed that's wrong since we were kids in Sunday school together, and now you're just trying to justify it in order to feel better about your actions."

As I watched an open, lively debate unfold, it struck me that this conversation could **never** happen between new friends. Not once did anyone's feelings get hurt, despite the seemingly brutal honesty. Not once did anyone do or say anything unloving. It's so important for each of us to develop relationships like that—with people we trust, people with whom we can openly admit our faults, people who know us well and love us anyway . . . no matter what.

So, do you have an idea of whom you'd like to draft for your team? Perhaps there are friends or family members who come to mind for you, and they're already a part of your life—that's great! Or maybe some acquaintances have popped into your head while you've been reading—people you want to get to know better or girls who you think will want to jump on board with you in working toward your mission. Talk to them and tell them what you hope to do, and then see if they'd like to join your team and change the world.

Keep 'Em on Your Team

Once you've cast your vision and inspired people to agree to work with you, there are a few things you need to know in order to *keep* them on your team. First, treat them well. Piero Soderini, a Renaissance leader in Florence, Italy, once wrote a letter to the Cardinal of Volterra, introducing a budding young artist: "Such is his nature that all may be gained of him, if one but speak kindly to him and show him friendliness. Given love and fair treatment, he will do things to astonish the whole world." [4] That artist was Michelangelo! If you can see the same world-changing potential in your teammates—and if you treat them that way—you'll be amazed at what you can do together!

Also make sure you're clear about your goals and about the position you'd like each person to play. People will get excited about your dream, but they'll quickly burn out if the roles you give them don't match their gifts. So try to help your teammates identify their own talents, passions, and interests, and then put them to work in a way that aligns with their strengths. That way they'll feel empowered, and they'll make a real difference.

Finally, be sure to pray regularly with and for your team. As we wrote this book, we prayed with each other every time we met together. We prayed for you (our readers), we prayed for our agent, and we prayed for our publisher. Most of all, we prayed that 1. God would be glorified; 2. he would keep our egos out of it; and 3. he would preserve our friendship through the writing process. Not a bad model for any team, if we do say so ourselves.

Find a Coach

A young friend of ours, Kristin, is passionate about horses. She's a pretty, tiny thing who boldly faces the taunting of rough men at the slaughter auctions just so she can rescue the horses she can afford to save. She also has a heart for kids. She knows a young girl with ADD whose family won't trust her with many responsibilities. Kristin taught her how to take care of and ride horses—now that little girl shows horses and wins awards! Kristin gave her the sense of immense satisfaction that only comes with hard work and responsibility.

Kristin's dream is to start a therapeutic horse farm that connects abused horses with abused kids. She believes that if those kids know their horse's story and they become responsible for caring for their own horse, that horse-rider relationship will begin to transform them. Though she knows a lot about horses, Kristin didn't know much about how to start such an ambitious project.

So what did Kristin do? She discovered a similar operation in Montana and has contacted the woman who runs it for help. She has found a coach. And now she can get started!

Sometimes it can be difficult to admit you need a coach—someone older than you who can give you a little guidance as you seek to live out your mission. Having a coach means that you need to be willing to listen and to follow her advice. Maybe you can identify with this bumper-sticker saying: "I don't have a problem with authority. I just don't like anyone telling me what to do." But King Solomon, said to be the wisest man who ever lived, offers you this advice:

- ๑ "Let the wise listen and add to their learning, and let the discerning get guidance" (Proverbs 1:5).
- ๑ "Plans fail for lack of counsel, but with many advisers they succeed" (Proverbs 15:22).
- ๑ "Listen to advice and accept instruction, and in the end you will be wise" (Proverbs 19:20).

If a wise king like Solomon wasn't above the need for the wise counsel of mentors and teammates, then neither are we!

No matter what your passion is—no matter what your skills are or how talented your team is—you need the help of someone who has gone before you and who can offer some wisdom and guidance to help you succeed. This mentor (or "coach," as we like to call it) can encourage you, help you stay on track, and enable you to network with other adults for resources they can provide. A coach can be someone from your church family, an aunt or a godparent, a youth group leader, a teacher, or your next-door neighbor—really any adult that stands out to you as someone who can show you the ropes and cheer you on.

What Does a Coach Do?

Andy Stanley says a coach should do three things: observe, instruct, and inspire. So if you want to get the most out of your coach, you've got to let her *inside*—you've got to let her really watch you at work. That's a little unnerving, isn't it? I mean, what if she thinks you're messing up? But the truth is, people are watching you all the time. Even if you're not asking for their input, they have their secret opinions anyway! You might as well find out what they're thinking so you can improve. Enlist the help of a wise person who cares about you and who wants to see you succeed. A good coach can help you see the girl God's created you to become.

How Do You Ask Someone to Be a Coach?

You don't.

"Wait a minute," you ask, "isn't that what you've just spent the last few paragraphs telling me to do? To *ask* someone to be my coach?"

Well, not exactly. We emphatically believe that you need a mentor—a coach. But we just don't think you should straight up *ask* them. Use the word "mentor" or "coach," and it'll likely freak them out! In fact, when we've been asked to be mentors, our immediate response was, *"Me? A mentor?!* I'm barely qualified to give myself advice, let alone you. Can't we just be . . . *friends?"*

If you directly ask an older woman to be your mentor or life coach, chances are she'll immediately think she's not qualified or she'll think it means a ton of work on her part. Either way she may be hesitant to jump on board. So instead start by asking for her help just one step at a time. If you're going to be leading a meeting, ask her to sit in on it. Tell her you respect her opinion and experience and that you'd like her to give you feedback on your style. Or if you're writing a fundraising letter you intend to send out, ask her to review it first and suggest changes. If you're about to give a presentation, ask her if you can practice it in front of her. Our point here is that people love to help and to give their input. When you approach your potential coach this way, she won't feel like she's committing to some huge undertaking, and you're not committing yourself either in case you feel later like it's not working out. But over time, the more she's given you constructive input and the more she gets involved in your efforts, she will naturally have become your coach . . . without the word ever having come up.

Two (Three, Four, Five . . .) Are Better Than One

Whether it's to celebrate our successes, to share in our pain, to encourage us when the going gets tough, or to come alongside us in helping us to achieve our dreams, we all need a team and a coach. We shouldn't try to do it alone. Ecclesiastes 4:9, 10 tells us,

> Two are better than one,
> because they have a good return for their work:
> If one falls down,
> his friend can help him up.
> But pity the man who falls
> and has no one to help him up!

Take time to pause in your dream to change the world and build a team around you with a strong coach to cheer you on. As you do, you'll see God's kingdom advance here on earth the way he intended: through the body of Christ.

Get Your Shoes on!

Questions for Small Group Reflection

Read these questions and talk about them with your friends—or jot down your own thoughts in your *One Girl Journal*.

1. Are you the kind of person who likes to do things on your own? Or do you most often rely on others? Tell a bit about which description best fits your personality and how that's played a role, positively or negatively, in your life so far.

2. Take a moment to reflect on how God has used others in your life so far to help you grow and become the person you are today. Who stands out in your mind as someone God has used powerfully to cheer you on and help you grow? Describe that person.

3. Think about a big accomplishment you've had in your life—something you're proud of. Now think about the team of people who helped you get there. Their involvement may be obvious to you or it may have been behind the scenes (like parents praying for you!). How did others play a key role in your success? How might things have turned out differently without that team?

4. Think of some women you know that you look up to and admire. Could any of them be a coach in your life? Share how you might want to get one of them involved in helping you grow and achieve your goals.

Time-out

how am i doing?

> "Winning doesn't always mean being first.
> Winning means you're doing better
> than you've ever done before."
> —Bonnie Blair, Olympic speed skater [1]

Am I Measuring Up?

From the time you're born, people start sizing you up. In the delivery room, after the nurses cleaned all the goo off you and your parents *oohed* and *ahhed* at your precious little wrinkled face, what was the next thing they did? They counted all your fingers and toes. "Yep, she's got ten of each!" Then, after you were fed and tucked restfully in the nursery and your mother had her first sleep after hours of labor, your dad started making phone calls to friends and relatives. When he proudly announced, "It's a girl!," what was the next thing nearly every recipient of that phone call asked? "How much does she weigh? How long is she?"

When you became a toddler and your mom met up with the other mothers at the playground, the conversation probably went something like this: "Is she crawling yet?" "Has she said her first word?" "Does she know her ABCs?" "Is she potty trained?"

Then you started school and you were measured in a different way: report cards. You're riding the school bus home and you know it's the day the report card is supposed to be in the mailbox. Your stomach is in a knot. Your palms are sweaty. You don't hear the conversation around you because you're dreading the dinner table talk.

Or maybe you were one of those weird kids (like Kim was!) who actually loved getting her report card. Maybe you like benchmarks—because they give you a chance to see how you're doing. Report cards or other evaluations help you see how you measure up and help you focus on how you want to improve.

The reality is that from the moment you were born, you've lived in a world of benchmarks and you'll continue being sized up for the rest of your life! So instead of just relying on others to take stock of you, take a moment right now for a time-out with yourself and God to see how you've been measuring up. By now you've hopefully begun taking steps in an area where you'd like to see the world changed. So stop right now and consider: Are you making a difference? Are you having influence? Are people excited and on board with you? Are you accomplishing the things you set out to do when you wrote your goals and objectives?

Kim: When my little brother was about seven or eight years old, he caught a couple of fish. They were small, but my mom believed in encouragement, so she cleaned them and wrapped them up and put them in the freezer until we needed just a few more to have enough for an actual meal.

A few weeks later, the preacher and his wife paid an unexpected visit to our house. My mom noticed that while the preacher's wife sat in our orange and brown tweed recliner (it was the '70s!), she seemed sort of uncomfortable. She'd squirm from time to time and wrinkle her nose, but kept a smile on her face and conversed politely.

After they left, my mom went over to the recliner to check it out and see if something was wrong. Right away she noticed a funny smell coming from it. She lifted the cushion and found my brother's thawed fish! He had been so proud of his catch that he couldn't bear the thought of our family eating them. So he'd hidden his treasure.

It's the same way with your spiritual gifts—if you hide them, you're just causing a stink.

The next three chapters are about overcoming some common obstacles that might trip up your progress or might tempt you to hide your leadership gifts. So as you continue reading along, keep these three steps in mind to help you measure your progress:

1. Review your plan.

Go back to your journal and revisit the dreams you wrote down and the commitments you've made. Are you achieving your goals? Does your mission statement still fit or does it need to be revised based on some things you've learned by now? If it needs to be revised, go ahead and change it!

2. Seek input from others.

Check in with your team, your coach, and your family members or other close friends to see how they think you're doing. If you've hit some roadblocks, talk about them. Your team can offer encouragement and feedback. Put your ego aside and listen with an open mind, even if their words are tough to hear. Be humble enough to admit your mistakes.

3. Make adjustments.

The Greek philosopher Aristotle once said, "We are what we

repeatedly do." [2] Stop doing the things that aren't working and keep the things that are.

In 1884 Amy Carmichael was sixteen years old and sitting in a tea shop eating dessert with her mother. She saw a little girl in a ragged and dirty dress standing barefoot outside in the rain, looking in at the sweets. Feeling a strong calling to help children like that little girl, Amy went home that night and wrote on the inside of her Bible:

> When I grow up and money have,
> I know what I will do,
> I'll build a great big lovely place
> For little girls like you. [3]

By the time Amy was twenty-seven (and for fifty-six more years), she was leading the Dohnavur Fellowship in India—a group that had saved more than 1,000 children from temple sacrifices, prostitution, and poverty! Along the way Amy faced many obstacles and setbacks, but at the end of her life she remembered the little girl from the tea shop. She kept her focus and she realized her goal.

Like Amy, resolve to meet obstacles head on as *you* press on toward the goal God has called you to.

part 3

How Do I *Keep* Going?

"Teach believers with your life: by word,
by demeanor, by love, by faith, by integrity . . .
Cultivate these things. Immerse yourself in them.
The people will all see you mature right before their eyes!
Keep a firm grasp on both your character
and your teaching. Don't be diverted. Just keep at it"
(1 Timothy 4:12, 15, 16, *The Message*).

8

catfighters and backbiters

> "Calling somebody else fat
> won't make you any skinnier.
> Calling someone stupid
> doesn't make you any smarter.
> And ruining Regina George's life
> definitely didn't make me any happier.
> All you can do in life is try to solve
> the problem in front of you."
> —Cady in *Mean Girls* [1]

> "God blesses those who work for peace,
> for they will be called the children of God"
> (Matthew 5:9, *NLT*).

In the movie *Mean Girls*, Cady Heron (played by Lindsay Lohan) has moved from the African jungle where she was homeschooled to a public high school in suburban Chicago. Now she has to learn how to survive the complex social rules of high school cliques. In one scene, exhausted by all the sneaky gossip, backbiting, and rumors, she imagines herself leaping across the cafeteria table at her nemesis, queen bee Regina George. The cafeteria becomes a jungle, and the two girls become like animals, pouncing on each other, claws out, hair wildly thrown over their faces, growling and gnashing—a true catfight. We watch this scene and think, "Ah, if only it were that easy to settle our differences!"

If you spend time with any girl of any age and in any place (and you are both breathing), you *will* experience conflict. Whether you've ever been in a bona fide catfight or you've just experienced a bit of cattiness here and there, you know what we're talking about. Resolving those inevitable conflicts is *not* easy. For one thing, young people today aren't often shown how to resolve differences in a healthy way. You watch adults try to hide their differences under the rug, thinking that by doing so they're keeping the peace. You're taught that it's "not ladylike" to speak up and confront issues head-on. Or on the flip side, you see women handle conflict by being cruel, sneaky, unkind, and vicious.

But being able to resolve conflicts is one of the most important skills you can learn. To change the world you've got to master conflict management. The good news is that Jesus gives us a perfect formula—but we'll get to it in a moment. First let's look at the most common causes of conflict between girls.

A First-Century Catfight

In the apostle Paul's letter to the Philippians, a church he loved, he wrote about two women who were not getting along. (With names like Euodia and Syntyche, it's little wonder they were grumpy!) It seems, after reading Paul's letter and knowing what we know about women, there must have been a lot of talk buzzing around about their fight. Evidently there was so much "she said/she said" going on that the gossip reached all the way to Paul, who was in prison in Rome! Some things never change. Even without e-mail or cell phone technology, juicy gossip travels fast.

So Paul begged them to work it out. Can't you just picture him pulling on his beard, throwing up his hands in exasperation, saying, "For crying out loud!"? *The Message* puts it this way: "I urge Euodia and Syntyche to iron out their differences and make up. God doesn't want his children holding grudges." And these women were world changers! Paul says they "contended at my side in the cause of the gospel." He then asks another friend to help Euodia and Synctyche get along (Philippians 4:2, 3). Who knows what started the conflict between Euodia and Syntyche? It could have been anything from a "she said that you said," to a "she started it/told it/took it/looked it/changed it," or even a "she rolled her eyes at me!"

Did you ever stop to wonder why we call conflict between girls a "catfight"? Girls who fight do, indeed, resemble mad cats. When two cats are going at it, it isn't pretty. There's a lot of hissing, scratching, meowing, fur flying, nails clawing, and deep wounding. More often, though, girls wound each other deeply on an *emotional* level. As Cady explained during the jungle scene in *Mean Girls,* "In Girl World, all the fighting had to be sneaky." In her book *Odd Girl Out,* Rachel Simmons explains that, "Girls use backbiting, exclusion, rumors, name-calling, and manipulation to inflict psychological pain on targeted victims."[2]

Kim: I once taught a lesson called "No More Mean Girls!" to a group of fifth- and sixth-grade girls. We talked about how girls fight differently than boys. Where boys will just punch each other and get it over with, girls hurt in other ways. I asked the girls to shout out all the mean things girls do to each other. I couldn't even keep up with my writing on the chalkboard as they shouted out mean things in rapid-fire succession. They said stuff like . . .

1. Rumors

2. Whispering

3. Eye rolling, giving the evil eye, staring

4. Writing nasty notes or text messages

5. Gossip

6. Ignoring (Isn't that one of the worst? Every girl knows the sick feeling of having to sit alone at recess or lunch.)

7. Emotional blackmail ("Do this or I won't be your friend anymore" or "If you invite her, then we can't be friends.")

8. Recruiting other people not to like someone

9. Acting fake/two-faced

10. Telling private jokes

11. Telling your secrets

12. Talking behind your back/backbiting

13. Secret name-calling

And that's just the beginning! Let's face it—we girls can **really** hurt each other.

This list puts our stomachs in knots. What about you? Have you ever been the subject of a rumor or been excluded by a group you thought were friends? Have you ever been a victim of psychological pain? We've all been there. In the Bible James zeroed in on the root cause of this kind of cruelty; he wrote, "What causes fights and quarrels among you? Don't they come from your desires that battle within you? You want something but don't get it" (James 4:1, 2).

The Green-Eyed Monster

What are those desires within that make us want what we think we do not have? Bob Sorge explains that the root of this green-eyed monster within can be found in one word: *envy*. In his book *Envy,* he claims that jealousy is the root of most of our conflicts, saying we "envy each other for such things as physical appearance, popularity and social status."[3] Uh . . . no kidding! We've all been there. When we let envy slip into our lives and allow it to permeate our hearts, it triggers all kinds of other problems like gossip, quarrels, fights, selfishness, slander, and bitterness.

Claudia: *I was recently at a local fast-food restaurant, and I watched a child clamoring for a kid's meal. Her mom said, "You will not have a kid's meal today—just a hamburger." The preschooler saw another child with a kid's meal and began to yell out, "She has one! I want one! She has one! I want one!" The child then threw a royal hissy fit, and her mom ended up carrying her, still kicking and screaming, to the car.*

So when it was my turn to place an order, I said, "I'll have the kid's meal." (I couldn't help myself. I wanted to see what that child felt so passionately about!) When I received my order, I read the message imprinted on the cup. It told me I could have things my way at this restaurant! It then listed all the different options I might choose for my drink.

The prize inside the kid's meal was an ugly creature with green scales and big black eyes. The directions, titled "Sulkers' Secret," said: "Place the sulker near a light, and see his eyes light up. Lower his left arm and his chest plate will pop off to reveal the real sulkers inside."

This is no joke. The teaching points that day were *soooooo* obvious! Right after watching a child totally lose her cool, driven mad by envy, I got to read the most obvious messages (that permeate our culture). When we aim to have our way in life, we become secret sulkers—ugly phantoms, looking around and asking God, "What about me? She has one! I want one too!"

At a conference one time, author and speaker Nancy Ortberg summed up the Christian's response to envy by saying that we just need to "get over our silly selves." In John 21, Jesus encouraged his disciple Peter to feed his sheep (in other words, to care for his people). Jesus then told Peter about how Peter would die. You'd think this would be very interesting to Peter, but instead he seems distracted. Look what he does in verse 20: "Peter turned and saw that the disciple whom Jesus loved was following them . . . When Peter saw him, he asked, 'Lord what about him?' Jesus answered, 'If I want him to remain alive until I return, *what is that to you?* You must follow me'" (John 21:20, 21, italics added). In other words, "Peter, get over your silly self."

So often we look around and envy the girls we see. Like Peter, we ask, "What about her, Lord? She (fill-in-the-blank: is so smart/is pretty/is talented/has a better family/is more popular/can eat anything she wants). What about her?" And Jesus answers us the same way he answered Peter: "What is that to you? *You* follow me." Get over your silly self.

Choice Morsels

One of the most damaging effects of envy is gossip. So let's talk nitty gritty here—what *is* gossip? Is it ever OK to talk about someone behind her back? When we praise someone to another person or ask others to pray for her (being careful not to share intimate details that the other person would not want made public), those are perfectly respectful ways of talking about another person. Gossip, on the other hand, is idle talk about someone else for your own selfish gain—whether it's to be popular, to build yourself up, to bring harm to another, to entertain yourself, or just to avoid more meaningful conversation.

We tend to think of gossip as nasty, dirty, and ugly, but the truth is that when we're in the middle of it, gossip is delicious. Proverbs 18:8 says, "The words of a gossip are like choice morsels; they go down to a man's inmost parts." It's hard to walk away from choice morsels like "Did you hear . . . ?" "Do you know about so-and-so . . . ?" "You won't believe . . ." or—the ever-so-subtle Christianized form of gossip: "We really need to pray for so-and-so. She's going through . . ."

Gossip is so mass-produced and commercialized that we often don't even recognize it when we hear it or see it. Think about how we wait in the doctor's office as we pour through the gossip-dripping magazines that invite us like choice morsels. Can you recite the names of J-Lo's twins? Who is Miley Cyrus's current boyfriend? Can you describe by heart Beyonce's latest red-carpet dress? Are Zac and Vanessa still together? If you can answer at least three of these questions, you gotta ask yourself if maybe you know too much! We see gossip everywhere, plastered on magazines and making the headline news. So it's no wonder that it just seems normal—unnoticeable—when we do it too. But it goes down—way down—into our innermost parts.

Rosalind Wiseman, author of *Queen Bees and Wannabees* (the book on which the movie *Mean Girls* is based), was interviewed on the *Today* show. When asked why she thinks we gossip, Wiseman cited a lack of confidence and a lack of substance in our own lives. She also said we use gossip to help us bond with other girls. Wiseman said we have to ask ourselves, "What am I getting out of it?" and then figure out how to get *that* without gossiping. [4]

We can be free from envy just as quickly as we remember that God's love is limitless—God has enough love for every person on this planet. For you *and* for those other girls you're tempted to envy. If you are in a "What about her?" mood right now, pause a moment and picture Jesus looking you in the eye and saying, "What's that to you? I have enough love and favor for you—there is no limit to it! Get over your silly self." To be a world changer you must get this idea about God's boundless love into your mind and heart. Satan wants to plant the root of envy. Thinking about God's boundless love will pull it up every time.

Can't We All Just Get Along?

When Abbey (a high school student) decided to host a girls' Bible study, the last role she expected to play in a group of Christian girls was the mediator of catfights. But no sooner had she received the final RSVP than the first phone call came in: "What about so-and-so? Is she coming?"

When Abbey said yes, the caller went into a long list of reasons why she didn't like this other person and why she didn't think she should be invited. While Abbey also had some hang-ups about certain members of the group, she also knew she was facing an important decision: "I could either agree with this girl and talk about who in the group I had problems with," she says, "or I could take a leadership role." She chose her words carefully before replying, "I know the group isn't perfect, but maybe this will be a chance for you to get to know her better . . . for us *all* to get to know each other better." After more convincing from Abbey, the caller agreed to give it a whirl and that maybe, just maybe, she could view the study as a chance to grow closer to God.

That was just the first hurdle Abbey had to deal with. She received a slew of phone calls from other girls talking about how they didn't like particular group members, how they thought a particular person was judgmental or another was bossy. The older girls looked down on the younger girls, and the younger girls were intimidated by the older girls. This was not the exciting start to her Bible study group that she'd wanted to have!

Abbey felt caught in the middle. After listening to so many complaints, she determined even more strongly *not* to voice her own negative thoughts. "Instead," she says, "through the grace of God, I talked to the concerned girls about trusting in the Lord to lead our study." Here's how Abbey explains what she did next:

"I encouraged the others to use this study as a chance to strengthen their faith and mend these strained relationships. (Where was I getting these words? It didn't sound like me.) I boldly told the other girls not to let these negative thoughts take hold of them but to come with an open heart. I encouraged them to use this opportunity to display a Christian attitude.

"I prayed about the group—I had to, I couldn't handle it on my own—and the Lord gave me the right words and the right heart. I listened with patience and understanding while they voiced their concerns, and then I turned the conversations around to God and his plan for the group. Even my friend that wanted to start the group in the first place started to have doubts. I felt really alone. I needed to trust God for this leadership role that he had seemingly placed me in. But he didn't expect me to do it alone; he equipped me for the job.

"I learned so much from helping organize this Bible study. The Lord really used this group to strengthen my walk with him. I never dreamed that the role of organizing this group would demand so much from me—but I learned that a leadership role comes with great responsibility and not to take it lightly.

"Leaders must be ready, first and foremost, to be obedient to God's Word and his leading. Leaders must also deal wisely with all different types of personalities, calm fears, ease tension, and not give in to their own negative thoughts but be an example to the people they are leading. We cannot do this on our own, but the Lord is ready and willing to help in the same way he helped me become a leader in this situation.

"As Christians we step into a leadership role when we are around non-Christians. We are leaders by our witness and examples to people who don't know Jesus, and the way we act and speak can have a great influence on people for the Lord. If we're leading a Bible study or a friend to the Lord, we need to exhibit biblical leadership qualities. But don't worry, because we have the best leader of all—Jesus Christ!" [5]

Follow Jesus' Prescription

Kim: One of my favorite memories from the girls' camp we run actually started out as a catfight—the sneaky kind. It all began when one camper gave another camper a funny look. Then one thought the other was whispering about her. Then one was making fun of the other's physical attributes. Then it escalated to name-calling and rumors. Before we knew it, the conflict between these two preteen girls had divided many of the rest of the campers into one side or the other. Throughout the day campers would hear amazing stuff about world-changing hearts, world-changing attitudes, and world-changing friendships, and then they'd go right back to whispering, gossiping, and name-calling!

And that's how I found myself on only the second night of camp in tears at one o'clock in the morning, ready to pull my hair out. I poured out my frustrations to my friend Cynthia.

Cynthia listened politely as I ranted: "We're here to learn about loving God and loving others, for crying out loud! Why can't they just get over it?!" Cynthia is a mother, licensed counselor, and children's minister . . . so she knows just a bit about conflict mediation. When I was done letting off steam, Cynthia smiled at me and said, "Well if we're going to expect them to live out Matthew 18, we need to model it for them."

OK. I'll admit it—I didn't have that one memorized. "Um, yeah, what's Matthew 18?" I asked.

So we reached for the Bible and read it together: "If your brother sins against you, go and show him his fault, just between the two of you. If he listens to you, you have won your brother over. But if he will not listen, take one or two others along, so that 'every matter may be established by the testimony of two or three witnesses'" (Matthew 18:15, 16). Basically the point here is pretty clear: there is absolutely no room for gossip.

The next morning I pulled aside Andrea and Kate, the high school girls who were in charge of leading the two campers who were in the big fight. I asked them to read the passage, and we talked about how they could use the conflict as a teaching opportunity. They planned to lovingly confront the two campers that night and explain to them that though their conflict was common for girls their age, Jesus had a perfect example of how we're to resolve conflict with our Christian sisters. Andrea and Kate planned to read the passage to the girls, talk it through, and then pray with them.

So after campfire that night, Andrea and Kate carried out the plan while I was busy supervising bedtime for the other girls. Later, as I was tucking a camper in, I heard Andrea's voice behind me. "Kim, we need to talk." I turned and saw both Andrea and Kate in tears. **Oh no!** I thought. **The situation is getting even worse!**

So we went outside where we could talk in private, and as soon as we were out the door, Andrea and Kate began jumping up and down exclaiming, "It works! It works!" Their tears were tears of joy. I was dumbstruck as they told me the story of how they had done exactly as planned and that, by the end of their conversation, the two enemy campers were crying and hugging. Those two campers were arm-in-arm the rest of the week, all was at peace, and we all were blown away by the power of God's Word to work in everyday life.

For your benefit, here are step-by-step instructions for following Jesus' prescription for resolving conflict:

1. **Pray.** Before you go, pray. It may also be helpful to write out and memorize what you want to say.

2. **Go.** If you hear something that your sister in Christ said or did that hurt your feelings, go directly to her and tell her. Forget e-mail and text messaging. Ephesians 4:26, 27 says, "Do not let the sun go down while you are still angry, and do not give the devil a foothold." Don't give the issue time to brew in your mind. Just go and get face-to-face and tell her what is hurting you. (Just remember that it's face-to-face and not "in your

face"!) Don't wait for the perfect time. It's *always* the right time, and it's always your turn.

3. **Keep it just between the two of you.** Notice that Jesus said the first conversation should be "just between the two of you." Don't take anyone with you. We girls don't even like to go to the bathroom alone, but now is not the time to have a third party add fuel for the fire. Involving someone else can only feed the gossip monster! This is a private matter between the two of you.

4. **Talk it out.** Start the discussion with an "I" message to explain your feelings. Use phrases like, "I felt hurt because I heard that you said . . ." But *don't* say exaggerated things like "you always" or "you never" when you speak—that will just make the fight bigger. Admit and apologize for any part you've had in the conflict. Work toward understanding each other. As Rosalind Wiseman says, "Your whole life is transformed when you can actually speak your mind."[6]

5. **Decide to "get over your silly self."** Sometimes the face-to-face problem solving will successfully lead to a deeper friendship, as it did with the two campers. Sometimes your sister will be shocked that she unknowingly hurt you, and you'll find that it was all a huge misunderstanding. But that doesn't always happen. Sometimes the other person will stay mad. If that happens, you've got to decide to ignore the offense and let it go. You may need to just agree to disagree and try to focus on the things you have in common.

One of the most dramatic stories we've ever heard about conflict resolution involved the young leaders of two rival gangs. Our friend runs the alternative school where both guys had ended up. These guys weren't into catfights—they were used to *shooting* at each other . . . literally! Needless to say, being together at the same school was causing quite a bit of conflict. So our friend sat them both down and told them clearly that they would have to find a way to get along or else both would be expelled. Basically this school was the last stop before jail for both of them; getting expelled would've changed the whole course of their lives.

Our friend discovered that both guys loved basketball, so he put them in charge of leading their community basketball team *together*. Through God's work in their lives, these guys found a way to work together, and their team eventually won the local tournament! A picture of the two former enemies appeared in the paper, holding their trophy together above their heads. Now those two guys are best friends and give talks at school fund-raisers on how Christ has changed their lives.

In the same way, Paul told Euodia and Syntyche to "agree with each other in the Lord" (Philippians 4:2). The Greek word for "agree" is *phroneo,* meaning to "direct one's mind to . . . to seek, to strive for." [7] In other words, these ladies were to change their attitude by putting their focus on Christ and not themselves. They just had to get over their silly selves and make up!

"Here there is no Greek or Jew,
circumcised or uncircumcised, barbarian,
Scythian, slave or free, but Christ is all, and is in all.
Therefore, as God's chosen people,
holy and dearly loved, clothe yourselves
with compassion, kindness, humility,
gentleness and patience. Bear with each other
and forgive whatever grievances
you may have against one another.
Forgive as the Lord forgave you.
And over all these virtues put on love,
which binds them all together in perfect unity"
(Colossians 3:11-14).

Get Your Shoes On!

Questions for Small Group Reflection

Read these questions and talk about them with your friends—or jot down your own thoughts in your *One Girl Journal*.

1. Look back at the list of things girls do to start conflict with each other (on p.150). How have you experienced these things? When have you been on the receiving end of these hurtful behaviors? When have you participated in doing some of these things? How do these behaviors affect you?

2. What factors can cause someone to be a "mean girl"? Explain.

3. Think about a time when you've gossiped. How did it make you feel? Do you agree with Rosalind Wiseman that gossip shows a lack of self-confidence or lack of substance in our own lives and that it's just a way for us to bond and feel popular? Explain why or why not.

4. Look again at the conflict resolution steps on p.158. Why do you think people usually *don't* handle conflict this way?

5. Are there any situations *you* need to address using Jesus' model of conflict resolution? How are these conflicts hindering your efforts to live out your God-given mission for your life? What do you feel God may be prompting you to do to make the situation right?

9

just keep swimming

> "You were running a good race.
> Who cut in on you and kept you
> from obeying the truth? That kind of persuasion
> does not come from the one who calls you"
> (Galatians 5:7, 8).

Our friend Savanna is the captain of her swimming team at Wellesley College. If you met her, we guarantee it would take under five minutes for you to discover how much she *loves* swimming. The fastest swimmer on her team, she was really looking forward to the conference championships—the highlight of three years' worth of work in collegiate swimming. But recently she was in a devastating bike wreck that resulted in two broken bones in her arm and a lot of soft tissue damage. After four hours of surgery (which included the screwing of metal plates on both bones), Savanna learned something even more devastating than the excruciating physical trauma itself: the wreck had ruined her season—no more competitive swimming . . . it was *all over.*

Kim recently talked with her by phone as she was walking back from class one night. They talked about the accident, what it has meant to Savanna, how she's handling the news, and where she'll go from here. "Ten seconds of my life ended up changing my future," Savanna said.

The swim team had competed in three meets since the accident, and it was really difficult for Savanna. She *really* wanted to be in the water competing, and ever since the accident there have been moments when reality hits her hard and leaves her feeling mad, upset, and scared.

But through it all, Savanna's been realizing firsthand the benefit of having a good coach and a good team. While she was in the hospital, her coach brought up the idea of Savanna helping to coach the team. Savanna said, "I'm not sure if she was serious, but I latched on to that. I'm the captain, and I'm not leaving my team . . . So I decided to set new goals." She and her teammates brainstormed about how to turn this huge obstacle in Savanna's life into an opportunity. They decided that two of Savanna's gifts are her swimming technique and her gift of encouragement. "Just because I can't swim doesn't mean my teammates don't love me and that I can't contribute," she told Kim. "We don't learn if we're not challenged."

Savanna feels like God is doing things in her life that she never would have dreamed of before her accident. Because she'd like to try to swim again next year, she's thinking of spending her fifth year at college getting a teaching certificate. She's thinking of taking a mission trip to Honduras and really wants to improve her Spanish. She also wants to spend some time in France teaching English. Despite the heartache, she's also excited about what God has in store. She told Kim, "I'm still who I am, and I'm still going for the best—even if it's something different." But as for exactly what that *something* different will be, she says, "I think leaving it up to God is a pretty good idea."

Perseverance

When you sign on to be a world changer, you can be *sure* there will be obstacles along the way. Sometimes unexpected circumstances, like what happened to Savanna, will threaten to detour you from your life mission. Other people, like catfighters and backbiters—and even well-meaning people who love you—can be roadblocks. Sometimes you'll face speed bumps like a lack of resources. Sometimes *you* will even be your own barrier. Lyn St. James, the second woman in history to race in the Indianapolis 500, knows a little about obstacles. She says, "Whenever I get to a low point, I go back to the basics. I ask myself, 'Why am I doing this?' It comes down to passion." [1] And that passion drives her to keep going, no matter what gets in her way.

The Bible calls it *perseverance*. When we think about perseverance, our friend Kara comes to mind right away. She's an all-around high achiever—but it doesn't always come easy. When at first she didn't make her high school basketball team, Kara didn't give up. She offered to serve as the team manager while she worked on developing her skills. The next time around Kara tried out again and *made* the basketball team. She worked hard, she was patient, she stayed focused. And her perseverance added to her already strong character.

Perseverance isn't simply "not giving up." Julie Andrews, the actress who played Mia's grandmother in *The Princess Diaries* and who's an accomplished stage actor and singer, believes that "Perseverance is failing nineteen times and succeeding the twentieth."[2] In typical paradox fashion the Bible says we should view our obstacles as gifts because they produce perseverance, which in turn produces character (Romans 5:3, 4). James 1:2-4 says, "Consider it pure joy, my brothers, whenever you face trials of many kinds, because you know that the testing of your faith develops perseverance. Perseverance must finish its work so that you may be mature and complete, not lacking anything."

So get ready to persevere because there will be obstacles in your way, like . . .

Obstacle 1: The Critics

Kaylee is on the honor roll and an athlete in multiple sports at her junior high school. She's the kind of girl who could write her own ticket to just about anywhere and become just about anything she chooses to be. But she already has a plan for her life, and she hasn't wavered for two years. She's planning to apply for a softball scholarship to a certain university where she wants to major in criminal justice and social work. Her dream is to be either a prison chaplain or to work with youth who are headed for the juvenile delinquent system. Sounds very noble, doesn't it? At least that's what *we* think. But some of her own relatives criticize her decision. "You won't make any money!" they say. "That's dangerous!" "You're wasting your talent." The people who should be most supportive of Kaylee are the ones throwing wet blankets on her dreams!

Ever been there? As we saw in the last chapter, people can sometimes be your biggest obstacles in life. Maybe they just don't like you or they feel threatened by your enthusiasm or they're just plain envious. Or maybe they're people who really love you but who want you to live out *their* dreams for your life rather than your own God-given mission. So what do you do about it?

First, recognize that you're in good company. Luke 6:22, 23 (*The Message*) says:

> Count yourself blessed every time someone cuts you
> down or throws you out, every time someone smears or
> blackens your name to discredit me. What it means is that
> the truth is too close for comfort and that that person is
> uncomfortable. You can be glad when that happens—skip
> like a lamb, if you like!—for even though they don't like
> it, I do . . . and all heaven applauds. And know that you

are in good company; my preachers and witnesses have always been treated like this.

World changers have always been persecuted. Read *Foxe's Christian Martyrs of the World* to get just a taste of the real dangers women have risked for their convictions. Perpetua, for example, was a twenty-six-year-old mother living in northern Africa in AD 200 who refused to make sacrifices to idols. When she was brought before the judge, her father was there, holding her baby and begging her to denounce her faith for the sake of her baby. The judge told her, "Spare the gray hairs of your father. Spare your child. Offer sacrifice for the welfare of the emperor." But Perpetua refused—she would *not* deny her commitment to Jesus, no matter what the cost. Because of her unwavering faith, despite the critics (even her own dad!), Perpetua was executed in the coliseum by a gladiator. [3]

Or how about these world-changing women? In 1527 Wendelmuta, a widow living in Holland, was arrested for her Christian beliefs. When she wouldn't renounce her faith, she was burned at the stake, holding a packet of gunpowder to her chest. [4] Joan Waste was a blind woman who bought a New Testament and hired a man to read it to her until she could commit entire chapters to memory. She was burned at the stake for her faith in 1556. [5] In third century Rome a young noble woman named Martina was beheaded for her commitment to Jesus. [6] Quinta, another world-changing woman, "was dragged by her feet over sharp flint stones, scourged with whips, and finally stoned to death" for her commitment to Jesus. [7]

Before you protest that these examples are all from ancient history, get your hands on a copy of Rebecca St. James's *Sister Freaks: Stories of Women Who Gave Up Everything for God*. It's full of examples of modern-day world changers facing very real obstacles. We know of a young woman, Mary, who's the daughter of our missionary friends in Myanmar.

She prayed that God would use her life "no matter what." While on a recent mission trip, she contracted malaria and nearly died. Mary was a faithful testimony to all who came in contact with her while she struggled for her life. As the Buddhist doctors and nurses were nearly ready to give up (they had lost a young boy to malaria a week before), they were shocked to find that her family's prayers to the "Christian God" were answered!

Somehow being criticized and made fun of doesn't seem like such a big deal now, does it? It's unlikely that you'll ever face mortal danger for changing the world in your area of influence. More than likely, the persecution you'll face will be from critics and naysayers, not prison guards. When you face persecution, be it verbal criticism or something worse, remember this verse: "Consider [Jesus] who endured such opposition from sinful men, so that you will not grow weary and lose heart. In your struggle against sin, you have not yet resisted to the point of shedding your blood" (Hebrews 12:3, 4). Kind of puts things in perspective, doesn't it? Since Christ endured the cross, and others are risking their very lives even today, let that embolden *you* to take on adventures where the stakes are much less risky.

Consider the Source

Eleanor Roosevelt once said, "Never allow a person to tell you no who doesn't have the power to say yes."[8] Nehemiah faced critics big time when he was rebuilding Jerusalem. His enemies criticized him and tried to distract him. They sent messengers five different times to try to get him to stop the work. They spread gossip saying that he was plotting a revolt and planning to set himself up as king (Nehemiah 6:6, 7). He sent back this reply: "Nothing like what you are saying is happening; you are just making it up out of your head" (Nehemiah 6:8). When Shemaiah tried to convince him to stop the work and hide inside the temple,

Nehemiah responded, in essence, "I realized God had not sent him, so I refused to stop working." (See Nehemiah 6:10-13.)

Follow Nehemiah's example: When you're facing off with critics and naysayers, consider the source. Test their objections to see if they are from God. What's behind their criticism? Is it personal? Do they have a problem with you? Is it envy? Or do they have a legitimate point? If they believe in your dream and can help you, listen to their logic. They may actually have some good points!

Obstacle 2: Well-Meaning People

Sometimes people put up obstacles because they *care* about you. They may think you've fallen off the deep end and want to bring you back to shallow waters. Because they love you, they want you to play it safe.

Kim: For longer than I can remember, a big dream of mine was to travel to Israel. I wanted to see firsthand the land of the God of the Bible! Israel pulled on my heartstrings for a very long time until, a few years ago, I happened upon an incredible opportunity to go.

But when I started telling people, some of my family members and friends freaked out. "It's not safe!" they told me. "You could be **bombed!**" I tried to assure them that it was actually very safe where I was going and that the people leading the group had been to Israel twice a year for the past fifteen years. My tour guide on the trip would be a highly decorated former general of the Israeli army!

My friends and family members had a good motive, born out of their love for me. **But this was my dream.** I believed firmly that I was to go. So I told my concerned friends and family members that even if I **did** die on this trip, I wanted them to know that I died doing something I loved. I told them that if I passed up this opportunity to go, I knew I'd always regret it. And what kind of a life is a life of regret?

And you know what? God incredibly blessed my decision. He spoke very personal things to me on that trip that I desperately needed to hear. I grew in my knowledge of him, and he has used that experience to bless others.

OK, now a quick note here about parents. This is a tough one because it's their *job* to keep you safe! When Kim faced a conflict between her family and her dream of traveling to Israel, she was a grown woman— her relationship with them was different than yours might be if you're still in your teens or living at home.

There may be times when you feel like your family is holding you back from your dreams. If you still live under your parents' roof—and even as you're transitioning to life on your own—you need to try to strike a delicate balance. Along with following your own God-given dreams, the Lord also calls you to *honor* and *obey* your parents. In other words, it's not going to please God if you defy your parents in your efforts to follow him! If you find yourself in a tough spot with your parents as a barrier between you and your dreams, talk it over with your coach or another spiritually mature Christian adult. Ask that person to help you navigate the best way through the situation as you honor God by honoring Mom and Dad. It may mean you have to put some specifics of your dream on the back burner for now—and that's OK. You've got a lifetime ahead of you to live out your dreams!

Even if people—parents, siblings, friends—don't agree with you, they will still be attracted to your passion and curious about your motives. Your willingness to take risks could very well draw people to the God who enables you to take those risks! When Paul was in chains in Rome at the end of his life, he wrote to the Philippian church in Philippians 1:12-14:

> Now I want you to know, brothers, that what has happened to me has really served to advance the gospel. As a result, it has become clear throughout the whole palace guard and to everyone else that I am in chains for Christ. Because of my chains, most of the brothers in the Lord have been encouraged to speak the word of God more courageously and fearlessly.

Many people, including some in Caesar's household, were converted to the faith because of how Paul handled his obstacles. May we, like Paul, see the opportunities in our obstacles.

Obstacle 3: Fear of Failure

If you've read much of the Bible, then you've seen that many of the people God called to do big things were *afraid!* Moses was afraid—"I am slow of speech and tongue" (Exodus 4:10). Jeremiah was afraid—"I do not know how to speak; I am only a child" (Jeremiah 1:6). Gideon was afraid—"I am the least in my family" (Judges 6:15). Elijah was afraid—"I have had enough, LORD" (1 Kings 19:4). David was afraid—"How can I ever bring the ark of God to me?" (1 Chronicles 13:12). Nehemiah was afraid—"I was very much afraid" (Nehemiah 2:2). Peter was afraid—"Lord, save me!" (Matthew 14:30). The ten spies sent with Joshua and Caleb to scout out the promised land were afraid, and their fear turned an eleven-day trip into forty years of wandering in the desert (Numbers 13).

But what did God tell Joshua after those forty years when he was getting ready to finally claim the promised land? Three times God told him, "Be strong and courageous" (Joshua 1:6). OK, sounds great. But have you ever had someone just *tell* you not to be afraid? It doesn't exactly take away your fear, does it? So *how* can we be strong and courageous? Here's how: God tells us, "Fear not, for I have redeemed you; I have summoned you by name; you are mine" (Isaiah 43:1).

Now *that* we can work with. It's the difference between someone saying, "Suck it up—it's only a haunted house" versus hearing your dad say, "It's OK, honey. I've got you. I'm going to carry you through it" and knowing you can hide your face in his chest all the way through. When you face fear, remember this amazing truth from God: "So do not fear, for *I am with you;* do not be dismayed, for I am your God. I will strengthen you and help you; I will uphold you with my righteous right hand (Isaiah 41:10, italics added).

The first time the Israelites were to enter the promised land, they chickened out—the inhabitants of the land were big and strong and intimidating. So when it was time for the Israelites to cross into the promised land the second time around, those big obstacles were still there. The difference was that *this* time they'd decided to trust God to carry them through. The truth is that our obstacles usually seem much bigger than they really are. Like the Canaanites seemed to the ten spies, they can make us feel like small little grasshoppers (Numbers 13:33). So just *do* the thing anyway! Eleanor Roosevelt once said, "You gain strength, courage, and confidence by every experience in which you really stop to look fear in the face . . .You must do the thing you think you cannot do." [9]

Try making a list of all the things you would have missed out on in your life if you'd listened to the voice of fear and not stepped out in courage. We'd have missed high school, riding a bike, riding a roller coaster, our first dates, learning to drive, snorkeling, and fly fishing within sight of a two-thousand-pound bison, to name a few. If Kim had listened to the fears of family and friends, she would have missed a boat ride on the Sea of Galilee, praying in the same garden where Jesus prayed the night he was arrested, walking in the tunnels under Jerusalem's Western Wall, drinking hot tea with Bedouins at Petra, and watching the sun set over Mt. Sinai.

If you don't face your fears, you're going to miss out on some great adventures.

Obstacle 4: Perfectionism

Perfectionism is closely tied to the fear of failure. It's that sense of waiting until you have every single detail checked off your list before you'll go for it. You know what we're talking about. It's the analysis paralysis that will stop you in your tracks because you fear you won't get it perfect.

Kim: I recently spent some time talking to a friend of mine about a big career change I feel God might be calling me to. I rattled off all the reasons why I shouldn't do it, not the least of which was, "What if I can't be great at it? I'll be starting all over, and it could take me years to be an expert in a new field." I thought I was just being a perfectionist, but my friend (who's really wise and who also just happens to be a psychologist) said, "Excuse me if this is direct, but I'm going to call that what it is: pure **pride**." Ouch! That stung . . . but I had to admit that she was right. My excuses were about wanting the outcome to glorify **me**—not about serving God. That conversation taught me an important lesson that I want to share with you too: God wants you to trust in *his* ability more than he wants you to get it perfect. He wants to show you something about **himself**.

When the Israelites were crossing into the promised land, God miraculously dried up the Jordan River. At God's command, the priests stood in the river holding the ark of the covenant until all of the people had crossed. Joshua 4:23, 24 says:

> The LORD your God dried up the Jordan before you until you had crossed over. The LORD your God did to the Jordan just what he had done to the Red Sea when he dried it up before us until we had crossed over. He did this so that all the peoples of the earth might know that the hand of the LORD is powerful and so that you might always fear the LORD your God.

He loves to show off. He loves to do things that cause everyone around you to stand in amazement with their jaws dropped, going, "How'd you do *that?!*" and to hear you say, "I didn't do it . . . *God* did."

Obstacle 5: Circumstances

When Amanda was nine years old, her mother was diagnosed with breast cancer. For a couple of years, her mother was too sick to take care of Amanda and her sisters, so they were passed around to a different family on a daily basis. Watching her mother endure operations, chemotherapy, and radiation, Amanda grew up quick. She was soon cooking, cleaning, doing laundry, and providing emotional support to her mother. When her younger sisters were scared or missed their mom, she held them while they cried and let them sleep in her room. On top of all that responsibility, Amanda was a good student and a top-notch volleyball player.

Even after her mother's cancer went into remission, she kept up the role of caretaker. When her parents' marriage started to disintegrate, she became her mother's listening ear and a shelter for her sisters when their parents fought. At a very young age, Amanda began to feel old—all the pressures and responsibilities on her shoulders were taking a toll and really wearing her out. It became difficult to keep up her grades. She felt like she had very few real friends. She felt *alone*.

Things came to a head when she had a bad hair day. She'd gone to the hair stylist with the goal of getting a haircut like the most popular girl in school—a straight bob that would swing between her ears and chin. But with her curly hair, it just turned out boyish and unruly. She went to church that Sunday feeling very ugly. She looked at the popular, smart, beautiful girls around her and felt overwhelmed. Something in her broke. She began to feel like her life was totally out of control. Tears started to fill her eyes. She ran to the bathroom and started crying. She suddenly felt that she could no longer carry the heavy burdens that were weighing her down.

Up until that point Amanda never wanted to admit that she couldn't handle it all on her own. For the first time that day, she told God that she needed his help more than anything. She told him she wasn't brave enough or smart enough without him. She told him she needed help with her grades, with her mother and sisters, with volleyball, with friends, and—yes—she even asked God to please make her hair grow miraculously right there in the bathroom.

Amanda explains, "My hair didn't change. But my heart did. I felt a sweet sense of peace and relief as I felt him take all my burdens and replace them with his unconditional love. The changes that he made in me were changes that made me feel beautiful, unique, and stronger. I don't know why I was so afraid that he would change me. He only changed me for the better." Amanda admits her life hasn't been perfect since then. She's still had to face many challenges, but through it all she has never been alone. She says that if a girl wants to be a world changer, she has to let God help. She has to admit that she can't do it without him. [10]

Sometimes it's not people or fear or perfectionism that presents the obstacles. Sometimes it's circumstances that have happened to you, through no fault of your own. So what do you do when you've got life-sized problems trying to hold you down? If you're facing difficult circumstances like Amanda's, seek help from a trusted adult immediately. While you *can* change the world, there are some burdens that you are not meant to carry at this age, and you are certainly not meant to endure your circumstances alone!

Next, do what Amanda did. Depend entirely on God's strength. Bruce Barton, founder of one of the most successful advertising companies in the twentieth century, said, "Nothing splendid has ever been achieved except by those who dared believe that something inside them was superior to circumstances."[11] Bruce Barton was a Christian, so we don't think it's a coincidence that his words sound so much like 1 John 4:4: "Greater is he who is in you than he that is in the world" (*KJV*).

And when awful circumstances come along, hold on to your own dreams! God is ironic sometimes—what you might view as a setback, God just may be using to shape you into the person you are meant to be! When Clara Barton was eleven years old, her brother fell from their barn, and she ended up spending the next two years taking care of him. Later Clara became a nurse—she's remembered in history for her care of Civil War soldiers. That world changer organized the American Red Cross! Those two heart-wrenching years in Clara's life, caring for her brother, prepared her to one day care for hundreds of people. When it comes to awful circumstances, Dr. Lloyd John Ogilvie (former chaplain of the U.S. Senate) says it well: "Hold fast to the vision God has given you for your life. The difficult things we go through are to prepare us for the realization of the vision on God's timing and by His power! I will not deny the vision that God has given me even when circumstances seem to contradict it!"[12]

A Smart Little Fish

In that great Disney flick *Finding Nemo*, Marlin finds himself facing terribly daunting circumstances. His son has been taken away, and it seems Marlin will never find him. So he's really, really discouraged—and understandably so! His somewhat annoyingly chipper (and air-headed) friend Dory asks Marlin, "When life gets you down, wanna know what you gotta do?"

But then she answers her own question with a surprisingly *smart* answer: "Just keep swimming. Just keep swimming, swimming, swimming."[13]

Remember Savanna? She's going to keep swimming. Despite the obstacles in her way, she's surrendered herself to God's will. Yes, literally speaking, she wants to recover from her injuries and keep swimming. But emotionally and spiritually and mentally she's *swimming now.* Her situation has changed—it's tough! But she hasn't given in to discouragement. Instead she's turned to God for help and is putting her energies in a new direction: encouraging others.

Since God has given us our passions and wants to see us accomplish great things for him, it may seem like he should just miraculously remove the obstacles in our lives. But he doesn't operate that way. In the same way that he left the obstacles in the promised land when the Israelites finally crossed over, he allows our obstacles to sharpen our skills and to develop our character. He also longs to delight you by showing you how mighty and powerful he is in the impossible circumstances you may face.

So when obstacles try to take you out of the pool—try to get you to give up your dream—view them with a different perspective! Hang in there . . . keep swimming . . . no matter what.

Get Your Shoes On!

Questions for Small Group Reflection

Read these questions and talk about them with your friends—or jot down your own thoughts in your *One Girl Journal.*

1. Describe a time when you faced obstacles in your life. What happened? How did God help you overcome them?

2. Paul, when he was in a Roman prison, was able to say that his obstacles had actually served as a testimony to draw others to Christ! How has God used obstacles in your life as opportunities to make a difference in the world or to touch others' lives? Explain.

3. We believe that if you don't face your fears, you're going to miss out on some great adventures in life! What's one fear in your life that threatens to hold you back from an adventure?

4. Do you struggle with perfectionism? If so, what are some details you need to let go of so you can just do the thing?

5. Who are some people in your life you can turn to during hard times? Are you willing to ask them for help if you need it? Why or why not?

10

blowing it big time

> "Here I should like to remark, for the sake
> of princes and princesses in general, that it is
> a low and contemptible thing to refuse
> to confess a fault, or even an error.
> If a true princess has done wrong, she is
> always uneasy until she has had
> an opportunity of throwing the wrongness
> away from her by saying: 'I did it; and I wish I had not;
> and I am sorry for having done it.'"
> —George MacDonald in *The Princess and the Goblin* [1]

> "My brokenness is a better bridge for
> people than my pretend wholeness ever was."
> —Sheila Walsh [2]

When you set out to change the world, don't be surprised by the roadblocks and detours in your path or the catfighters, backbiters, critics, and naysayers that try to hold you back. Don't be surprised when fear or perfectionism threatens to stall your progress. Don't be surprised if you end up going through some huge unforeseen circumstance, like Savanna, with a tough experience like a physical injury throwing a wrench (or, in her case, a metal plate) in your plans.

And *especially* don't be surprised if you end up just blowing it big time.

What we've discovered is that sometimes *we* are our own obstacles. You know what we mean, right? Think about it for a minute. What have *you* done to get your plans off track? Have you let your grades slip because you're putting more emphasis on your social life? Have you neglected the importance of the work you do now for reaching your future dreams? Have you done something to damage your reputation or a relationship? Or perhaps you're just not living up to your own expectations, even though you know you're capable of more? How have you blown it big time?

Claudia: When I taught first grade, my friend Linda taught a class called pre-first. These were students who had completed kindergarten but were just not quite ready for first grade. A boy named Jason was in Linda's class. Jason was a kid who always wanted a hug. The problem was, he seemed to have a perpetual string of snot hanging from his nose. So I'd just try to pat Jason on the head when he lunged at me with open arms. Linda, however, would embrace him like she didn't even notice.

One day Jason brought a toy hammer to school. He took the yellow hammer out of his pocket and began to hammer on everything—the wall, the desks, the other students. My friend Linda told him, "Jason, that hammer has a sharp point on it. It could hurt someone. Better put it away." Jason had a good heart. Obeying his teacher, he tucked the hammer in his good jacket pocket.

Soon it was recess time. With two hundred children, they called it "Nightmare on Playground Street." On this particular day, I didn't have recess duty, so I was grading papers at my desk when I suddenly heard loud screaming coming from the playground. Jason had climbed to the top of the tornado slide and taken the hammer out of his jacket pocket, swinging it round and round. It had accidentally slipped out of his hand and flown across the playground, striking a first grader just above her eyebrow. She had blood running down her face and was screaming along with a choir of two hundred other screaming first graders.

My friend Linda reached for the wounded child with one hand, the "criminal" Jason with the other, and headed for the school building. When she reached my classroom and saw me at my desk, she led Jason into my room and asked me to watch him while she took the other child to the nurse. Sobbing with big tears rolling down his cheeks, Jason kept saying over and over, "I want my teacher! I want my teacher!" **(Kid, you're crazy!** I thought. **When your teacher gets back, you are in for some big trouble!)** Then he said, "Mrs. Mitchell, I think I'm going to throw up." And that's when I said, "Let's find your teacher."

What happened next changed my life. When we spotted Jason's teacher at the end of a very long hallway, he went running to her with tears rolling down his cheeks. Linda saw him and ran toward him with her arms outstretched. She dropped to her knees and hugged him. She said, "It's OK, Jason. I know you didn't mean to hurt her. She's OK; she just needed a bandage." Where **I** expected to see him punished, Linda offered him love and forgiveness. I watched in amazement and prayed out loud, "God help me be like my friend. **Help me to see hearts and not hammers.**" Immediately a thought came to me that I knew was from God: **Claudia, every single day I see your heart and not your hammer.**

Our friend Lilly, now a college student, heard the Jason story as she grew up because we often told it at our summer camp for girls. It stuck with her, and recently, over a cup of coffee, she asked us, "Do you want to hear my own hammer story?" She'd been working at a popular upscale discount store where her job was to do the prep work in the restaurant area. She got so burned out from juggling a heavy school and work schedule that she ended up doing something totally out of character: she skipped work for three days in a row. She just didn't show up for her scheduled hours. She didn't even call to explain. This was a big deal! The restaurant depended on the prep work she did before hours in order to open to customers on time. And she blew it.

But the thing was, Lilly loved her boss. She says Gloria was like a surrogate mother to her and the last thing she wanted to do was to let Gloria down. But she had.

By the third day she felt so badly about it that she called the store and asked to speak with Gloria. When Gloria came to the phone, and before she could get out more than a "Hello?" Lilly blurted out an emotional, "I'm so sorry! I'm so sorry! I know what I did was horrible, and there's no excuse. I messed up."

Gloria's only response was a curt, "Can you come in tonight?" Lilly said, "Yes, yes, of course. I'll be there—anytime." They hung up and Lilly went to work in trepidation. Apologizing on the phone was one thing, but actually having to face Gloria in person would be another.

When she walked in and found Gloria organizing some merchandise at the end of an aisle, she tentatively approached her. Gloria turned to see her, smiled, and reached out her arms to Lilly. Not a word was said about the past three days. Gloria simply hugged her and said, "I'm so glad you came . . . Thank you for coming." Lilly cried as she thought of little Jason on the playground—she'd just experienced for herself what it really felt like to have someone see her heart and not her hammer.

A Life-Changing Look

The apostle Peter blew it big time—and it's documented in all four gospels to be read by generations to come. (And you thought the rumor mill at your school was bad!) You've probably heard the story of how Peter denied Jesus three times the night he was arrested. This friend of Jesus' who'd been with him throughout his ministry, who'd seen the miracles, who'd prayed with him in the Garden of Gethsemane, who'd pulled out his sword and cut off a man's ear to defend Jesus, later that same night did just as Jesus foretold and denied him!

We like the way Luke tells it. Luke doesn't let us just read the facts, shake our heads, and say, *"Tsk-tsk,* Peter, you should've known better!" Luke gives us an extra bit of information that causes us to pause and think about the emotion involved in that moment. As do the other Gospel writers, Luke paints a picture of Jesus having been arrested and taken to the high priest's house. Peter follows and gathers with the crowd around a fire in the courtyard. Three different people accuse of him of having been with Jesus, and three times he denies it. But here's where Luke adds something. Right there in Luke 22:61—after Peter's just denied Christ again, saying, "Man, I don't know what you are talking about!"—Luke says that "the Lord turned and looked straight at Peter."

What do you think was expressed in that look?

Think about a time you've messed up and immediately locked eyes with your mom or dad or a teacher or a friend. What did you see? hurt? disappointment? anger? forgiveness? Whatever Peter saw in Jesus' look, Luke tells us that right after he "went outside and wept bitterly" (Luke 22:62). You've surely been there. You've surely felt the bitter emotions that come from having blown it big time.

Whatever else was conveyed in the look Jesus gave Peter, you can be sure of one thing: it included love. We used to read that story and end with the "and he went outside and wept bitterly" part. But the story doesn't end there. You see, after the resurrection, Jesus makes a visit to Peter. You have to turn to John 21 to catch it. Peter has been fishing from a boat with some other disciples. They've been out all night with no luck. It's now morning, and Jesus is on the shore frying up some fish. He calls out to them, "Friends, haven't you any fish?" They don't recognize him at first, until he tells them to throw the net on the right side of the boat and they catch so many that they can't haul in the net. As soon as another disciple recognizes Jesus and says to Peter, "It is the Lord!", Peter *jumps* into the water and swims and then runs to Jesus. We can only imagine what that reunion was like for Peter, but we bet it was something like when Linda hugged Jason or when Gloria hugged Lilly. Were Peter here with us today, he'd surely tell us about the amazing time Jesus saw his heart and not his hammer.

We don't know what you may be feeling as you read this book. Perhaps you feel wounded, depressed, alone, burdened, or unloved. Maybe you're disappointed in who you are or what you've done. Maybe, like Peter, you've blown it big time. You've done something you swore you'd never do or said some words you wish you could take back or just not lived up to your expectations of yourself. You may be feeling like you've been banged in the head a time or two, or maybe you've done your own share of hammer throwing. Like Jason, maybe you feel like you're about to throw up with the guilt of some sin. So what do you do?

Run to Jesus

First, take a lesson from Jason, whose only thought was *I want to see my teacher!* Just as Lilly could not rest until she talked with Gloria, neither can we rest until we fall on our faces and confess it to God, our teacher. James 4:10 promises, "Humble yourselves before the Lord, and he will lift you up."

God's Love is Now

Second, no matter what you are feeling right now, think this thought with us: *God loves me right in this moment, exactly as I am.* God loves us so much, and he wants us to run to him, just like Jason ran to his teacher— to run to him with all our hammers and our regrets. Jesus, who even loved the Jasons with the hammers that nailed him to the cross, loves *us* and invites us to lay our hammers down.

In spite of it all, Jesus sees your heart and not your hammer. Psalm 103:10-13 tells us this same idea in these poetic words:

> [God] does not treat us as our sins deserve
> or repay us according to our iniquities.
> For as high as the heavens are above the earth,
> so great is his love for those who fear him;
> as far as the east is from the west,
> so far has he removed our transgressions from us.
> As a father has compassion on his children,
> so the LORD has compassion on those who fear him.

Perhaps you're like a friend of ours who told us that he always had a very hard time *really* believing that God loved him unconditionally. He thought, *If God* really *knew me* (he laughs at the absurdity of that thought; of course God knows us!), *he couldn't possibly love me.* But then one day our friend got this very strong mental image of his own son in prison— wearing an orange jumpsuit and sitting behind a glass window waiting to talk to him by phone. As soon as our friend got this vision of his son, he thought, *What could he* possibly *have done to get himself there that would make me no longer love him?* And our friend told us, "You know, I couldn't think of anything my son would have done that would make me love him any less. In fact, I'd be doing everything I could to break down that glass to get to him." And he realized that's how God felt about *him.*

And you know what? That is how God feels about *you.* In fact, he did that very thing. He broke through the barrier to get to you, despite anything you've ever done or ever will do, in spite of the fact that he knows the *real* you. In *The Ragamuffin Gospel,* author Brennan Manning asks:

> "Do you really accept the message that God is head
> over heels in love with you? I believe that this question is
> at the core of our ability to mature and grow spiritually.
> If in our hearts we really don't believe that God loves us
> as we are, if we are still tainted by the lie that we can do
> something to make God love us more, we are rejecting the
> message of the cross."[3]

Zephaniah says, "The LORD your God is with you, he is mighty to save. He will take great delight in you, he will quiet you with his love, he will rejoice over you with singing" (3:17). Not *was* with you or *will be* with you. God *is* with you—loving you, rejoicing over you, right now as you are reading this page. Think this thought with us: *I am God's child, and he loves me right now, in this moment and in this place. I don't have to do anything or be anything. God just loves me.* And bask in this idea! Dance, sing, and shout with the understanding that, because of Jesus, God sees your heart and not your hammer!

Get Up!

Lastly, pick yourself up and move on! Look, we're all going to blow it at times. Don't let your hammer moments paralyze you from going forward and being what God intends you to be! After Jesus and the disciples had finished eating that morning on the shore, Jesus turned to Peter and asked, "Do you truly love me?" (John 21:15-17). He asked it three times. Jesus was driving the point home, knowing that Peter would still be guilt-ridden over denying him three times. Jesus knew that Peter really loved him. But, when Peter replied three times, "You know that I love you," what was Jesus' response? "Feed my lambs." "Take care of my sheep." Yes, Peter had made a mistake. But Jesus still had *work* for him to do. And no matter what you've done, sweet girl, he still has work for you to do too. Run to him, seek his forgiveness, bask in his love, and know that "he who began a good work in you will carry it on to completion" (Philippians 1:6).

Get Your Shoes On!

Questions for Small Group Reflection

Read these questions and talk about them with your friends—or jot down your own thoughts in your *One Girl Journal*.

1. Where do you see yourself in the Jason story? Are you the wounded child, the teacher, or one of the kids observing the crime from the playground? Explain why.

2. How do you picture God? Is he a policeman in Heaven waiting to catch you doing something wrong? Or is God the teacher who sees your heart and not your hammer? Explain.

3. Think about a time when you've blown it big time. (If you're comfortable sharing with the group, do so.) How did you react? Did you, like Jason, run straight to the arms of your teacher, or did you hide? What keeps us from going straight to Jesus when we've blown it?

4. Think about a time when a friend has blown it big time with you. Did you see her heart or her hammer? How could you have handled the situation differently? What do you need to do now to make it right?

5. James 4:10 says, "Humble yourselves before the Lord, and he will lift you up." Spend some time as a group on your knees together, humbled before the Lord. Confess your sins. Next, turn to your neighbor and say, "God loves you and forgives you."

conclusion

Get Your Shoes On!

> "Give a girl the correct footwear and
> she can conquer the world."
> —Bette Midler

Claudia: My dad was a preacher, and raising me provided him with an abundant supply of teaching opportunities. One of the most profound lessons he ever taught me has proven useful over and over again in my life. Whenever I'm facing a difficult project or obstacle, my mind replays the words that he'd often say to calm my anxious spirit.

The first time he said them, I was a freshman in high school and had decided to try out for the school musical. I **really** wanted it. I loved dancing. The production was my all-time favorite: **The Music Man.** (By the way, the guy I really wanted to date was also trying out.) But I was a nervous wreck. Many of my friends who I considered to be much more talented than me (including the reigning Junior Miss Indiana), were also trying out. My dad hired a dance coach to help me prepare, and I took voice lessons from the high school music teacher. I prepared a song from **The Sound of Music** for my audition, and I practiced 'til I knew the song and dance by heart.

Then the day of auditions came and I was a bundle of nerves. I suddenly felt like I couldn't do it. "Dad!" I moaned, "I **cannot** go through with this! My life is over!" Unmoved by the drama, my dad simply asked, "Honey, do you have your shoes on?" Suddenly I felt a sermon coming on and, sure enough, he grabbed a Bible and opened to Acts 12:6-8. He read:

> The night before Herod was to bring him to trial, Peter was sleeping between two soldiers, bound with two chains, and sentries stood guard at the entrance. Suddenly an angel of the Lord appeared and a light shone in the cell. He struck Peter on the side and woke him up. "Quick, get up!" he said, and the chains fell off Peter's wrists. Then the angel said to him, "Put on your clothes and sandals." And Peter did so.

My dad then asked me the question that led to a change in my life that remains to this very day. "Why do you think the angel, who had the ability to break Peter out of jail and make the chains fall off his wrists, would ask **him** to put on his shoes? Why didn't the angel put Peter's shoes on for him? Obviously, that extra step would have been no problem for the angel."

When it was obvious I didn't have an answer, my dad whispered, "**Because God wants us to do what we can, and he will perform the miracle.** Get your shoes on, Claudia. Do all you can do to prepare yourself, and God will perform a miracle like you cannot imagine."

I was able to pull myself together after that and my audition went great. I got a good part in the play . . . and the guy I liked was in it too and ended up asking me to prom! But the amazing thing for me has always been the conversation with my dad, not the results of the audition. Many times throughout the years, I've remembered that moment. I imagine my dad's arms around me, and it's like I hear him all over again, asking in his soft, firm voice, "Honey, do you have your shoes on?"

You've invested a good amount of time reading this book and (hopefully) doing the exercises to discover the leader you were born to be. We've hoped to convince you that you *can* change the world. Just one question remains: whether your style is Juicy Couture™ sandals, Converse® high-tops, Dr. Martens boots, Jimmy Choo platforms, or Manolo Blahnik heels, *will you get your shoes on?*

Long before she became a missionary, Amy Carmichael felt the call to "go forth" but had no idea how that call would be manifested in her life. Even in waiting for her specific instructions from God, she kept moving and doing—always with the conviction that her work was preparation for something bigger. She got her shoes on and waited for God to do the miraculous.

On April 25, 1893, when she was just twenty-five years old, Amy landed on the Japanese island of Honshu for her first foreign mission assignment.[1] She was far away from home and family. Rather than the privileged life she was accustomed to, she became as poor as the people she was sent to serve. She ate strange food, wore strange clothing, and struggled to learn a strange language. But along the way she won converts to Christ. Little did she know that, fifty-two years later, the nearby big city of Hiroshima would be destroyed by an atomic bomb. Like Jonah being sent to Nineveh years before its destruction, Amy was part of a movement to spread the love of Christ to an unreached country. But she didn't know that then, of course. She simply put her shoes on and let God do the miraculous.

Maybe for you it's not going to another country and saving thousands of children from poverty and prostitution. Maybe it's something closer to home, like bridging the gap between cliques at school or being a light to your own family. Maybe it's reaching out to the poor or homeless in your own community or teaching English to Spanish-speaking kids. Maybe you want to zero-in on a certain disease and raise money or awareness to advance a cure. Wherever God is stirring your heart, why not start with getting your shoes on? Sit next to the school outcast at lunch and get to know her. Clean the house for your mom (and when she asks why you did, tell her, "Just because I love you!"). Let your kid sister tag along the next time you go shopping. Gather up some canned goods and take them to the local food pantry. Visit with the elderly widow next door. Rent a hot dog stand at a local supermarket and donate the money you raise to your favorite cause. You get the idea! Get your soul shoes on every day and go forth with an attitude of service to others. Do the thing that's right in front of you—changing the world begins with the first small step.

Deuteronomy 29:5 tells us that when God was leading the Israelites through the desert, their sandals did not wear out . . . for forty years! In the same way, our prayer for you is that you will take what you've learned here and that your world-changing shoes will never wear out!

Get Your Shoes On!

Questions for Small Group Reflection

We've got just one more question for you to talk about in your small group or to write about in your *One Girl Journal:*

It's time for *you* to take your place on God's time line and change the world. What will it mean for you to "get your shoes on!"? What is the next thing you need to do?

We'd love to hear from you!

If *One Girl Can Change the World* inspires you, go to

www.onegirlcanchangetheworld.com

to check out ways other girls are changing the world around them.

endnotes

Introduction

    1. Will Rogers, http://www.brainyquote.com.

    2. Thomas A. Edison, http://www.brainyquote.com.

    3. Bette Midler, "Exclusive: Bette Midler Interviews the Divine Miss M," *After Dark*, May 1978, http://www.betteontheboards.com/boards/magazine-19.htm (accessed March 5, 2009).

Part 1 (quote)

    1. Lynne Hybels, *Nice Girls Don't Change the World* (Grand Rapids: Zondervan, 2005), back cover.

Chapter 1

    1. Quoted in John and Stasi Eldredge, *Captivating* (Nashville: Nelson Books, 2005), 186.

    2. Information from lexicon entry for *azar* from Blue Letter Bible, http://www.blueletterbible.org (accessed March 5, 2009).

    3. Frank T. Seekins, *A Mighty Warrior* (Phoenix: Living Word Pictures, Inc., 2004), 24.

    4. Nicole Johnson, *Keeping a Princess Heart: In a Not-So-Fairy-Tale World—A Conversation Guide for Women* (Nashville: W Publishing Group, 2004), 138.

    5. Erwin Raphael McManus, *The Barbarian Way* (Nashville, Nelson Books, 2005), 54.

    6. Dialogue from "Memorable Quotes for *Ever After*," *Internet Movie Database*, http://www.imdb.com (accessed March 5, 2009).

    7. Frances Hodgson Burnett, *A Little Princess* (New York: Penguin Books, 2002), 105-106.

8. Dialogue from "Memorable Quotes for *Princess Diaries 2: Royal Engagement*," *Internet Movie Database*, http://www.imdb.com (accessed March 5, 2009).

Chapter 2

1. Mark R. Schwehn and Dorothy C. Bass, eds. *Leading Lives that Matter* (Grand Rapids: William B. Eerdmans Publishing Company, 2006), 112.

2. Bruce Wilkinson, *The Dream Giver*. With David and Heather Kopp. (Sisters: Multnomah Publishers, Inc., 2003), 80-81.

3. Story used with permission of Lauren Gifreda.

4. Margaret Thatcher, http://thinkexist.com.

5. Leo Tolstoy, *Confession* (New York: W. W. Norton & Company, 1983), 75.

6. C. S. Lewis, *Mere Christianity* (New York: Simon & Schuster Inc., 1980), 176. *Mere Christianity* by C. S. Lewis copyright © C. S. Lewis Pte. Ltd. 1942, 1943, 1944, 1952. Extract reprinted with permission.

7. Laurie Beth Jones, *The Path* (New York: Hyperion, 1996), 3.

8. Ibid., xvii.

9. Dialogue from "Memorable Quotes for *City Slickers*," *Internet Movie Database*, http://www.imdb.com (accessed March 8, 2009).

10. Thomas à Kempis, *The Imitation of Christ* (New York: Catholic Book Publishing Co., 1993), 133.

Chapter 3

1. Story used with permission of Rita Delp.

2. John Trigilio and Kenneth Brighenti, *Women in the Bible for Dummies* (Indianapolis: Wiley Publishing, Inc., 2005), 141.

3. Corrie ten Boom, *The Hiding Place* (New York: Bantam Books, 1971), 197-199, 209.

4. Albert Einstein, http://thinkexist.com.

5. Meg Cabot, *The Princess Diaries* (New York: HarperCollins Publishers, 2000), 97-98.

6. Madeleine L'Engle, *A Wrinkle in Time* (New York: Dell Publishing, 1962), 84.

Part 2 (quote)

1. Dr. Seuss, http://thinkexist.com.

Chapter 4

1. Elisabeth Elliott, "CQ Daily Archives: February 2000," *The Timothy Report*, http://www.timothyreport.com/february2000.html (access February 3, 2009).

Chapter 5

1. Coco Chanel, http://thinkexist.com.

2. David and Pat Alexander, eds., *Zondervan Handbook to the Bible* (Grand Rapids: Zondervan Publishing House/Lion Publishing, 1999), 226.

3. Beth Moore, *Breaking Free: Making Liberty in Christ a Reality in Life* (Nashville: LifeWay Press, 1999), 160.

4. Stephen Ross, "Frances Ridley Havergal: Devotional Writer, Poetess and Hymn Writer," *Wholesome Words Christian Biography Resources,* http://www.wholesomewords.org/biography/bhavergal.html (accessed March 8, 2009).

5. Public Domain.

Chapter 6

1. Albert Schweitzer, http://www.brainyquote.com.

2. Dialogue from "Memorable Quotes for *My Big Fat Greek Wedding*," *Internet Movie Database*, http://www.imdb.com (accessed February 12, 2009).

3. Holly Brower, interview with author, January 12, 2006.

4. Andy Stanley, *The Next Generation Leader* (Sisters: Multnomah Publishers, 2003), 132-133.

5. Ibid., 155.

6. Story used with permission of Jessica Cassel.

7. Story used with permission of Kayla Castleberry.

8. Harry S. Truman, http://thinkexist.com.

Chapter 7

1. Mother Teresa, "Mother Teresa's Message to the UN's Fourth World Conference on Women," open letter written September 1995, http://www.ewtn.com/New_library/MT_woman.htm (accessed March 8, 2009).

2. Dialogue from "Memorable Quotes for *Lemony Snicket's A Series of Unfortunate Events*," *Internet Movie Database*, http://www.imdb.com (accessed March 8, 2009).

3. Dialogue from "Memorable Quotes for *Ever After*," *Internet Movie Database*, http://www.imdb.com (accessed March 9, 2009).

4. Georg Brandes, *Michelangelo: His Life, His Times, His Era*. Heinz Norden, trans. (New York: Frederick Ungar Publishing Co., 1963), 209. Also available online at http://ia311540.us.archive.org/2/items/michelangelohisl017905mbp/michelangelohisl017905mbp.pdf (accessed March 9, 2009).

Time-out

1. Bonnie Blair, http://www.brainyquote.com.

2. Aristotle, http://www.brainyquote.com.

3. Sam Wellman, *Amy Carmichael: For the Children of India* (Uhrichsville: Barbour Publishing, 1998), 22-23.

Chapter 8

1. Dialogue from "Memorable Quotes for *Mean Girls*," *Internet Movie Database*, http://www.imdb.com (accessed March 9, 2009).

2. Rachel Simmons, *Odd Girl Out: The Hidden Culture of Aggression in Girls* (New York: Harcourt, Inc., 2002), 3.

3. Bob Sorge, *Envy: The Enemy Within* (Ventura: Regal Books, 2003), 30.

4. Rosalind Wiseman, interview by Ann Curry and Hota Kotb, *The Today Show*, NBC, October 1, 2007.

5. "Abbey" is a pseudonym; the girl in this story wishes to remain anonymous. Story used with permission.

6. Rosalind Wiseman, interview by Ann Curry and Hota Kotb, *The Today Show,* NBC, October 1, 2007.

7. Lexicon entry for *phroneo* from Blue Letter Bible, http://www. blueletterbible.org (accessed February 7, 2009).

Chapter 9

1. Lyn St. James, http://www.quotemountain.com.

2. Julie Andrews, http://www.brainyquote.com.

3. John Foxe, *Foxe's Christian Martyrs of the World* (Uhrichsville: Barbour and Company, Inc., 1989), 13-14.

4. Ibid., 58.

5. Information from *Foxe's Book of Martyrs Variorum Edition Online,* http:// www.hrionline.ac.uk/johnfoxe/apparatus/person_glossaryW.html (accessed March 9, 2009).

6. John Foxe, *Foxe's Christian Martyrs of the World* (Uhrichsville: Barbour and Company, Inc., 1989), 14.

7. Ibid., 15.

8. Eleanor Roosevelt, http://thinkexist.com.

9. Eleanor Roosevelt, http://quotationspage.com.

10. Story used with permission of Amanda Kester.

11. Bruce Barton, http://www.brainyquote.com.

12. Lloyd John Ogilvie, *God's Best for My Life* (Eugene: Harvest House Publishers, 1997), 277.

13. Dialogue from "Memorable Quotes for *Finding Nemo,*" *Internet Movie Database*, http://www.imdb.com (accessed March 9, 2009).

Chapter 10

1. George MacDonald, *The Princess and the Goblin* (New York: Puffin Books, 1996), 200.

2. E-mail message to author from http://www.sheilawalsh.com, January 8, 2009.

3. Brennan Manning, *The Ragamuffin Gospel* (Sisters: Multnomah Publishers, Inc., 2000), 159.

Conclusion

1. Sam Wellman, *Amy Carmichael: For the Children of India* (Uhrichsville: Barbour Publishing, 1998), 59-60.

one girl can change the world

Every girl has a purpose.
Every girl is uniquely gifted.
God calls every girl to lead with her own style.

The One Girl series reminds young women that they have a specific role in impacting the world, inspires them to discover their passions and leadership styles, and encourages them to effectively live out their purpose. One Girl features biblical stories, popular culture, and principles that create a strong theological base for leadership that serves others.

One Girl Can
Change the World
978-0-7847-2229-9
$16.99

one girl
leader's guide
for planning events, retreats,
and small groups

mitchell & kim goad

One Girl
Leader's Guide
978-0-7847-2231-2
$19.99

one girl
journal

One Girl
Journal
978-0-7847-2230-5
$16.99

one
girl

**For more information or to order
call 1-800-543-1353 or visit
www.standardpub.com**